The Ridgeway

National Trail Companion

supported by

The
Countryside
Agency

3rd edition published February 2004

© National Trails Office

ISBN 0-9535207-5-7

Edited by Jos Joslin & Rebecca Wilson

Published by

National Trails Office

Environment & Economy

Holton

Oxford OX33 1QQ

tel 01865 810224

fax 01865 810207

email mail@rway-tpath.demon.co.uk

website www.nationaltrail.co.uk

Produced by www.leap-frog.co.uk

Designed by Linda Francis

Cover photo:

Ivinghoe Beacon from Pitstone Hill

Contents

I	Introduction	5
II	History	8
III	Wildlife	9
IV	Using The Ridgeway	11
V	Finding Your Way	13
VI	Publications	15
VII	Tour Operators	16
VIII	Useful Contacts	17
IX	Getting There	21
X	Respect the Countryside	22
XI	Emergency Contacts	23
XII	Accommodation, Facilities & Services	25
●	Section 1 – Overton Hill to Uffington Castle	29
●	Section 2 – Uffington Castle to Streatley	47
●	Section 3 – Streatley to Chinnor	63
●	Section 4 – Chinnor to Ivinghoe Beacon	79
	Index of Places	95
	Distances between places	96

The Manger below Uffington Castle

Introduction

One hundred and thirty six kilometres (85 miles) long, much of it following the ancient chalk ridge route used by prehistoric man and surrounded by numerous historic monuments, The Ridgeway offers the chance to get away from the bustle of life in this busy part of England. Perfect, but not too strenuous, for long distance use, this Trail is also ideal for day trips or less. The whole of The Ridgeway can be enjoyed by walkers with horseriders and cyclists able to use all of the western half as far as the River Thames at Streatley and short sections further east.

The Ridgeway

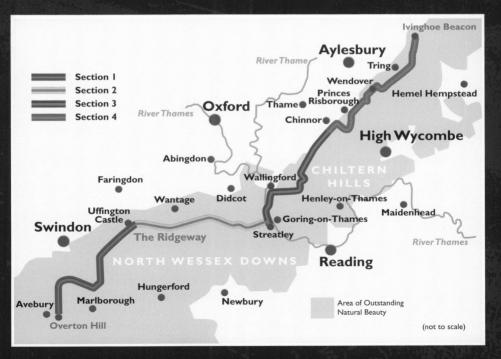

1 INTRODUCTION

Welcome to the Ridgeway Companion. It provides up-to-date practical information about accommodation, refreshments and many other facilities along this National Trail. The Companion is designed to help with planning anything from a week's holiday to a short walk or ride.

The Companion is not a route guide: for detailed information about the Trail itself, The Ridgeway National Trail Guide by Neil Curtis (Aurum Press, 2001) is available from most book shops or from Amazon via the internet. Alternatively it can be mail ordered from the National Trails Office (see page 17 for details). The Companion complements the Trail Guide and, armed with a copy of each, it is hoped that anyone using The Ridgeway needn't require anything more. Enjoy your trip.

One of only 15 National Trails in England and Wales, The Ridgeway starts in the famous World Heritage Site of Avebury in Wiltshire and travels for 136 km (85 miles) steadily north east along the surprisingly remote scarp ridge of the downs, across the River Thames, and through the Chiltern Hills to finish in the Iron Age fort on top of Ivinghoe Beacon in Buckinghamshire.

The western half of The Ridgeway, as far as Streatley-on-Thames, can be enjoyed by walkers, horseriders and cyclists, whereas only walkers can use the full extent of the eastern half. Despite its relative remoteness, public transport to The Ridgeway is pretty good, especially to the eastern half, where there are several railway stations close to the Trail and an excellent bus network. With a little planning many places along the western half can also be reached by bus or train or a combination of the two.

The Ridgeway passes through two distinctive protected landscapes, both designated Areas of Outstanding Natural Beauty (AONB). The western half of the Trail travels through the open expansive downland of the North Wessex Downs AONB, whilst east of the Thames it stays amongst the more gentle and wooded countryside of the Chiltern Hills AONB.

In the west The Ridgeway travels as a broad ancient track along the open and fairly isolated top of the chalk downland ridge, often several kilometres from the nearest village. Here, to the south is rolling downland and to the north, at the bottom of the steep scarp slope, the wide expanse of the Thames Valley. The far-reaching views are

dominated by the sky, the clouds and small clumps of beech woodland and all you may have for company is a solitary skylark singing overhead or a hare chasing across an adjacent field.

In the past these downs were sheep grazed, but since the introduction of fertilisers in the first half of the last century many areas have been ploughed and planted with crops. However sheep grazing does continue in places and, in others, a characteristic sight is immaculately managed grass tracks, the gallops used for training racehorses. The excellent turf of the downs makes this prime horse country but you need to be up early to see the strings of racehorses exercising.

At Streatley The Ridgeway crosses the River Thames, and another of England's National Trails, the Thames Path, entering more intimate and less open countryside. It follows the bank of this famous river along a lovely 8 km (5 miles) rural stretch before heading eastwards into the Chiltern Hills. Mostly on narrower paths, the Trail passes through woodlands, many of them beech, over neatly cultivated fields and across chalk grassland nature reserves rich in wildflowers. In contrast to the western half, although its usually peaceful here, you're never far from pleasant small towns or attractive villages.

With the support of the Countryside Agency, The Ridgeway is managed to the highest standards necessary for one of the most important paths in the country by the local highway authorities with a small dedicated team of staff.

Sheep on Pitstone Hill, Buckinghamshire

II HISTORY

For thousands of years, at least 5,000 and maybe many more, people have walked or ridden The Ridgeway, be they drovers, traders, invaders or today's recreational visitors. As part of a prehistoric track once stretching about 400 km (250 miles) from the Dorset coast to the Wash on the Norfolk coast, The Ridgeway provided a route over the high ground for travellers which was less wooded and drier than routes through the springline villages below.

New Stone Age men, the first farmers in Britain, left the earliest remains. Their long barrows can be found at a few places both west and east of the River Thames. It was Bronze Age people from later times, around 2,000 BC, however, who dragged the huge sarsen stones from the surrounding hills and formed the dramatic Avebury Circle. There are many of their round burial barrows along the length of the National Trail.

Wayland's Smithy, a New Stone Age long barrow 2 km (1.2 miles) southwest of Uffington Castle

Hill forts built during the Iron Age from about 500 BC until the Romans arrived in 43 AD are also found both sides of the Thames. These forts command the high ground and in several places they defended The Ridgeway against attack from the north.

In the Dark Ages The Ridgeway was a main route for the Saxons and Vikings who fought many battles during their advances into Wessex. In medieval times it was drovers driving livestock from Wales and the West Country to the Home Counties, not armies, who used The Ridgeway.

Until the Enclosure Acts of 1750 The Ridgeway was a broad band of tracks along the crest of the downs where travellers chose the driest or most convenient path. During Enclosures the exact course and width of The Ridgeway was defined by the building of earth banks and the planting of thorn hedges to prevent livestock straying into the newly cultivated fields.

In recent times use of The Ridgeway has changed greatly: farmers do still use much of it as an access route to their fields for tractors and other machinery but its main use is no longer utilitarian but recreational with walkers and riders out for exercise, pleasure and spiritual refreshment.

The grasslands which occur on the chalk of the downs and the Chiltern Hills are some of the most interesting habitats in England and some of the richest in terms of the number of plant species found. Chalk grassland has suffered from modern farming and much has disappeared under the plough. However those unimproved chalk grassland areas along The Ridgeway, especially the nature reserves east of the Thames, are well worth visiting where you'll find, amongst many other lovely plants, several types of orchid.

Another botanical treat in store for visitors during springtime is the carpet of bluebells in many of the woodlands in the Chiltern Hills, usually in the first couple of weeks of May.

For those keen on seeing birds, The Ridgeway should not disappoint you. A range of relatively common birds such as warblers and finches are found the length of The Ridgeway enjoying the food supply provided by the hedges lining the Trail. Skylarks, yellowhammers and corn buntings are particularly characteristic of the downland and although generally in decline in Britain are still fairly numerous along The Ridgeway.

The song of the corn bunting, likened to the sound of a jangle of keys, is the distinctive sound of the western half of The Ridgeway.

In colder months flocks of redwing and fieldfare, winter visitors from Scandinavia, are common and are usually seen feeding in the fields surrounding the Trail. However, most people will especially cherish the site of a red kite and you'll be unlucky if you don't see one in the Chiltern Hills. These magnificent birds of prey recognised by their forked tail were reintroduced to this area in the late 1980s and are now well established. In woodlands of this area too, woodpeckers and nuthatches may well be spotted.

Apart from the ubiquitous rabbit, hares and deer are the larger wild animals you may encounter. Hares are found in open countryside and are bigger than rabbits with longer ears and hind legs. They are solitary animals and most active at night, so late evening or early morning are the best times to see them. Two species of deer are found on The Ridgeway, roe and fallow with the former being the smaller and also living in smaller groups of just three or four animals. Both of these species are nocturnal and shy so, as for hares, being on The Ridgeway at dusk or dawn will give you the best chance of viewing them.

The Ridgeway provides excellent walking, cycling and horse riding opportunities although it is only walkers who can use the whole length of the Trail.

Cyclists and Horseriders

Riders, both cyclists and horseriders, can share The Ridgeway with walkers all the way from the start at Overton Hill near Avebury to Streatley on the River Thames, a distance of roughly 68 km (43 miles). Once across the river the only long section of the Trail which can be ridden is the 13 km (8 miles) stretch which follows the Icknield Way through the Chilterns from Britwell Hill near Watlington to Wainhill on the Oxfordshire/Buckinghamshire border. In other places The Ridgeway is a footpath and it is a trespass offence to ride on a footpath without the permission of the landowner.

However an alternative for riders is to join the Swan's Way long distance bridleway at Goring on Thames, just across the river from Streatley, and to follow this, mostly on The Ridgeway to Bledlow west of Princes Risborough (here the Swan's Way turns north). From Bledlow riders can pick up the Icknield Way Riders' Route which provides a good alternative to The Ridgeway for riders as far as Pitstone Hill, just a couple of kilometres from Ivinghoe Beacon. Unfortunately riders can't continue to Ivinghoe Beacon, the official end of the National Trail, since the route to it is on footpaths.

Vehicles

It's worth knowing, so that it doesn't come as a surprise to see a motorbike or four wheel drive, that vehicles can legally use most of the western half of The Ridgeway and a few sections east of the Thames. However recreational vehicles and motorcycles only comprise about 5% of the total usage of The Ridgeway with agricultural vehicles another 1%, so you're unlikely to meet too many vehicles.

Code of Respect

A Code of Respect has been operating on The Ridgeway for the last few years to encourage all users to act responsibly to conserve the Trail and to be aware and considerate of the rights of others. Details of the Code are shown on page 18 and you are asked to familiarise yourself with it before visiting The Ridgeway.

IV USING THE RIDGEWAY

Be prepared!

When venturing into the countryside it is wise to be prepared for the elements: even in summer, wind and rain can make a walk or ride cold and uncomfortable, so suitable warm and waterproof clothing should be worn or carried in a small rucksack. In the summer, especially on much of the western half of The Ridgeway which is exposed, it is also advisable to wear protection against the sun and to carry a water bottle since water points are relatively infrequent (see each section for information on these).

From April to the end of October most years The Ridgeway is usually dry with conditions on the whole good. There are, however, places where ruts have developed and care needs to be taken, so do wear strong, comfortable footwear. From November to March parts of The Ridgeway can become muddy making it difficult in places to walk or cycle - on the whole you'll find that the footpath sections are fine.

 ### Dog Matters

If you are planning to undertake a long distance walk along The Ridgeway with your dog, you are advised to ensure it is fit before you start; on occasions walkers have had to abandon a walk because their dogs can't keep up!

Please also make sure your dog is under close control at all times to prevent it from disturbing livestock or wildlife. You are asked to keep your dog on a lead when you're in the few fields you'll encounter with livestock, although if you find that cattle seriously harass you because of the dog, it may be wise to let it off the lead.

Signing

The Ridgeway follows a series of well-signed public rights of way along which people have legal right of access.

An acorn, the symbol of Britain's National Trails, is used to guide your journey by marking the route in a variety of ways. It is used in conjunction with coloured arrows or the words 'footpath', 'bridleway' or 'byway' to indicate who can use a particular right of way.

The word 'footpath' and/or a yellow arrow indicates a path for use by walkers only and where, without the landowner's permission, it is illegal to cycle, ride a horse or drive a vehicle.

The word 'bridleway' and/or a blue arrow indicates a path which can be used by walkers, horseriders and cyclists but where, without the landowner's permission, it is illegal to drive any vehicle.

The word 'byway' and/or a red arrow indicates a right of way which can be legally used by walkers, horseriders, cyclists and motorists.

The Ridgeway is signposted where it crosses roads and other rights of way using mostly recycled plastic materials. Elsewhere, waymark discs with acorns and coloured arrows are used on gates and waymark posts.

Guides

The Ridgeway National Trail Guide by Neil Curtis, Aurum Press, updated 2001 and costing £12.99 is the official guide with written route description and colour 1:25 000 maps.

Harvey Maps publish **Ridgeway**, a detailed waterproof map at the scale of 1: 40 000 of the entire National Trail which includes locations of facilities and services close to the Trail. It costs £8.95.

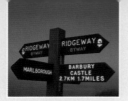

V FINDING YOUR WAY

Maps

It is usually a good idea to use maps when walking, particularly in unfamiliar areas. The National Trail Guide includes colour sections of all the appropriate 1:25 000 Ordnance Survey maps needed to follow The Ridgeway. Alternatively, for you to enjoy and interpret the wider landscape, you may wish to purchase your own Ordnance Survey maps.

The Landranger series (pink cover at 1:50 000 or 2 cm to 1 km) has all public rights of way, viewpoints, tourist information and selected places of interest marked on them. For the whole of The Ridgeway you will need:

173	Swindon and Devizes
174	Newbury and Wantage
175	Reading and Windsor
165	Aylesbury and Leighton Buzzard

The larger scale Explorer series (orange cover at 1:25 000 or 4 cm to 1 km) has more detail including fence lines which can be very helpful when following rights of way, recreational routes and greater tourist information. For the whole of The Ridgeway you will need:

157	Marlborough and Savernake Forest
170	Abingdon, Wantage and Vale of White Horse
171	Chiltern Hills West
181	Chiltern Hills North

After harvest near Streatley

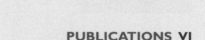

Publications About The Ridgeway

The Ridgeway National Trail Guide by Neil Curtis, Aurum Press, updated 2001 - the official guide with written route description from Overton Hill to Ivinghoe Beacon and colour 1:25 000 maps. Available from the National Trails Office.

Ridgeway, Harvey Maps, 1999 - 1:40 000 scale waterproof map of the entire route of The Ridgeway including information on a range of facilities along the Trail. Available from the National Trails Office.

Exploring the Ridgeway by Alan Charles, Countryside Books, updated 2000 - based on 14 circular walks covering the whole length of The Ridgeway from Ivinghoe Beacon to Overton Hill.

The Oldest Road - an Exploration of the Ridgeway by J R L Anderson with photographs by Fay Godwin, Wildwood House, 1975. Paperback edition by Whittet Books, 1992.

Walking in Britain, Lonely Planet, 2001 - includes a description of the western half of The Ridgeway.

The Greater Ridgeway by Ray Quinlan, Cicerone, 2003. Describes a route from Lyme Regis to Hunstanton, including The Ridgeway National Trail.

Ridgeway Routes Pack - leaflets describing circular and other walks from The Ridgeway. Available from the National Trails Office.

Ridgeway Circular Riding Routes Pack - leaflets describing circular rides from The Ridgeway. Available from the National Trails Office.

Let's Hear it for The Ridgeway! by Elizabeth Newbery - a family activity book full of ideas and information on things to do and see on and close to The Ridgeway. Available from the National Trails Office.

Ridgeway Public Transport Leaflet - details of bus and train services for the whole Trail. Free from the National Trails Office.

Events Programme - a range of guided events around The Ridgeway. Free from the National Trails Office.

VII TOUR OPERATORS

The following companies offer self-guided or guided holiday packages on part or all of The Ridgeway.

Walking

Contours Walking Holidays, Smith House, Stainton, Cumbria CA11 0ES. **T**: 01768 867539 www.contours.co.uk - 7-night self-guided package from £350.

Explore Britain, 6 George St, Ferryhill DL17 0DT. **T**: 071400 650900 www.xplorebritain.com - 9-night self-guided package from £522.

Cycling

Cycling Adventure Tours, Flat 4, Lexham Gardens, Kensington, London W8 5JB **T**: 020 7835 0288 www.venturetours.co.uk - free Sunday rides programme and a variety of holidays, sometimes including The Ridgeway.

Rough Tracks, Alexandra Road, Frome BA11 1LX. **T**: 07000 560749 www.rough-tracks.co.uk - weekand gudied tour in Wiltshire including part of The Ridgeway.

Horse Riding

Pewsey Vale Riding Centre, Church Road, Stanton St Bernard, Marlborough SN8 4LJ **T**: 01672 851400 - www.pewseyvaleridingcentre.com - 1 or 2-day ride from Pewsey to Streatley.

Bridle Rides Ltd, PO Box 9233, Bromsgrove B60 1PF. **T**: 0121 445 6998 www.bridlerides.co.uk - 2-5 day rides along the western half of The Ridgeway for those riding their own horse.

Please note for those visiting The Ridgeway independently many of the accommodation providers listed in this guide are willing to collect you from and return you to The Ridgeway. Many will also transport your luggage to your next night's accommodation.

The Ridgeway Managers

Mike Furness and Jos Joslin, National Trails Office, Environment & Economy, Holton, Oxford OX33 1QQ. **T**: 01865 810224. **F**: 01865 810207.
E: mail@rway-tpath.demon.co.uk

Highway Authorities responsible for public rights of way

Buckinghamshire County Council, Environmental Services Dept, County Hall, Walton Street, Aylesbury HP20 1UY. **T**: 01296 395000 www.buckscc.gov.uk

Hertfordshire County Council, Planning and Environment, County Hall, Hertford SG13 8DN. **T**: 01992 555555 www.hertscc.gov.uk

Oxfordshire County Council, Countryside Service, Cultural Services, Holton, Oxford OX33 1QQ. **T**: 01865 810226 www.oxfordshire.gov.uk

Swindon Borough Council, Borough Engineer's Dept, Premier House, Station Road, Swindon SN1 1TZ. **T**: 01793 463000 www.swindon.gov.uk

West Berkshire Council, Countryside and Environment, Faraday Road, Newbury RG14 2AF. **T**: 01635 42400 www.westberks.gov.uk

Wiltshire County Council, Dept of Environmental Services, County Hall, Trowbridge, Wilts BA14 8JD. **T**: 01225 713000 www.wiltshire.gov.uk

Agency responsible for National Trails

Countryside Agency, South East and London Region, Dacre House, 19 Dacre Street, London SW1H 0DH. **T**: 0207 3402900 www.countryside.gov.uk

Areas of Outstanding Natural Beauty

North Wessex Downs AONB Office, Denford Manor, Hungerford RG17 0UN.
T: 01488 685440 www.northwessexdowns.org.uk

Chiltern Hills AONB Office, 8 Summerleys Road, Princes Risborough HP27 9DT
T: 01844 271306 www.chilternsaonb.org

Code of Respect

To respect this National Trail so that it can be enjoyed by all, please ...

● Act responsibly to conserve The Ridgeway

● Be aware and considerate of the rights of others

	walker	cyclist	horserider	carriage driver	motorcyclist	driver – recreational four wheeled vehicle	driver – agricultural vehicle
FOR RECREATION YOU CAN							
Use all The Ridgeway	✓						
Use all except footpath sections		✓	✓				
Use all except footpath and bridleway sections				✓	✓	✓	
CODE OF RESPECT – YOU SHOULD							
Understand that others have legitimate access to many sections	✓	✓	✓	✓	✓	✓	✓
Spread the message about responsible care	✓	✓	✓	✓	✓	✓	✓
Follow the Country Code	✓	✓	✓	✓	✓	✓	✓
Limit your use when the surface is vulnerable during and after wet weather			✓	✓	✓	✓	✓
Avoid using The Ridgeway if you can find or develop another route							✓
Keep to well-used parts of the track to prevent damage to the whole width					✓	✓	✓
Continue to help by reinstating the surface where possible							✓
Make sure you and your vehicle are fully road-legal					✓	✓	
Make sure your bicycle is roadworthy		✓					
Drive at a quiet and careful speed with no more than 4 four-wheeled vehicles or 8 motorcycles in any one group					✓	✓	
Ride at a safe and controlled pace		✓	✓				
Help other users and make your own visit more enjoyable by using The Ridgeway when it is less busy					✓	✓	
Warn walkers of your approach and pass carefully			✓	✓			
Warn walkers and horseriders of your approach and give way to them		✓					
Give way to horseriders	✓	✓					
Watch out for and respect temporary voluntary restraint signs and report registration numbers of those who break codes to LARA (Motoring Organisations' Land Access & Recreation Association). Tel: 01630 657627					✓	✓	

KEY

● walker	
⚲ cyclist	
∪ horserider	
◉ carriage driver	
motorcyclist	
driver - recreational four wheeled vehicle	
driver - agricultural vehicle	

Organisations for walkers

Backpackers Club, c/o Peter & Carol Shiner, 117 Swinford Road, Selly Oak, Birmingham B29 5SH. **E**: pc@shiner117.freeserve.co.uk

Long Distance Walkers Association, Membership Secretary, 63, Yockley Close, Camberley GU15 1QQ **E**: membership@lwda.org.uk www.ldwa.org.uk

Oxford Fieldpaths Society, c/o Mr D Godfrey, 23 Hawkswell House, Hawkswell Gardens, Oxford OX2 7EX. **T**: 01865 514082 www.ofs.org.uk

Ramblers Association, 2nd Floor, Camelford House, 87-89 Albert Embankment, London SE1 7TW **T**: 020 7339 8500 www.ramblers.org.uk

Organisations for cyclists

British Cycling Federation, National Cycling Centre, Stuart Street, Manchester M11 4DQ. **T**: 0870 8712000 **E**: info@britishcycling.org.uk www.bfc.uk.com

Cyclists Touring Club (Off-Road), Cotterell House, 69 Meadrow, Godalming GU7 3HS. **T**: 0870 873 0060 **E**: cycling@ctc.org.uk www.ctc.org.uk

Sustrans, 35 King Street, Bristol BS1 4DZ. **T**: 0845 113 0065 **E**: info@sustrans.org.uk www.sustrans.org.uk

Organisations for horseriders

British Horse Society, Stoneleigh Deer Park, Kenilworth CV8 2XZ. **T**: 0870 120 2244 **E**: enquiries@bhs.org.uk www.bhs.org.uk

Byways & Bridleways Trust, PO Box 117, Newcastle upon Tyne NE3 5YT. **T**: 0191 2364086

Endurance GB, National Agricultural Centre, Stoneleigh Park, Kenilworth CV8 2RP. **T**: 02476 698863 **E**: enquiries@endurancegb.co.uk www.endurancegb.co.uk

VIII USEFUL CONTACTS

Other organisations

Berkshire, Buckinghamshire & Oxfordshire Wildlife Trust, The Lodge, 1 Armstrong Road, Littlemore, Oxford OX4 4XT. **T**: 01865 775476 **E**: bbowt@cix.co.uk www.wildlifetrust.org.uk/berksbucksoxon

Chiltern Society, White Hill Centre, Chesham, HP5 1AG. **T**: 01494 771250 **E**: office@chilternsociety.org.uk www.chilternsociety.org.uk

Friends of the Ridgeway, c/o Mr Peter Gould, 18 Hampton Park, Bristol BS6 6LH. **E**: Ridgewayfriends@aol.com www.ridgewayfriends.org.uk

Herts & Middlesex Wildlife Trust, Grebe House, St Michael's Street, St Albans AL3 4SN. **T**: 01727 858901 **E**: info@hmwt.org www.wildlifetrust.org.uk/herts

Wiltshire Wildlife Trust, Elm Tree Court, Long Street, Devizes, SN10 1NJ. **T**: 01380 725670 **E**: admin@wiltshirewildlife.org www.wiltshirewildlife.org

From Lodge Hill, southwest of Princes Risborough

Getting to The Ridgeway by public transport is fairly easy, particularly the eastern half of the Trail, and a useful map-based leaflet showing relevant public transport routes is available free from the National Trails Office (see page 16 for details).

Alternatively, telephone numbers and websites to find out more about public transport to the Trail are listed below:

• Rail Services   08457 484950 (24 hours a day)
                               www.nationalrail.co.uk

• Bus Services   0870 6082608
                               www.pti.org.uk

Information about taxi services is included in each of the four sections.

Those wishing to travel to The Ridgeway by car are asked to park considerately if parking in villages on or close to the Trail. Other places to park are listed within each section.

The Ridgeway Explorer

X RESPECT THE COUNTRYSIDE

• Enjoy the countryside, but remember that most of The Ridgeway crosses private farmland and estates which are living and working landscapes.

• Always keep to the Trail to avoid trespass and use gates and stiles to negotiate fences and hedges.

• Crops and animals are the farmer's livelihood - please leave them alone.

• To avoid injury or distress to farm animals and wildlife, keep your dogs under close control at all times - preferably on a lead through fields with farm animals (NB if you are concerned that cattle are harassing you, it may be safer to let your dog off the lead).

• Remember to leave things as they are - fasten those gates you find closed. Straying farm animals can cause damage and inconvenience.

• Please take your litter home, otherwise it can injure people and animals and looks unsightly.

• Guard against all risk of fires especially in dry weather.

• Take special care on country roads and, if travelling by car, park sensibly so as not to obstruct others or gateways.

The downs near Wantage

In emergency dial 999 and ask for the service required.

Police

To contact local police stations, telephone the number relevant to the section/county you are in and ask to be put through to the nearest police station.

Section	County	Tel Number
1	Wiltshire	01380 735735
	Oxfordshire	08458 505505
2	Oxfordshire & Berkshire	08458 505505
3	Oxfordshire	08458 505505
4	Oxfordshire & Buckinghamshire	08458 505505
	Hertfordshire	01707 354000

Grim's Ditch east of Wallingford during Spring

XI EMERGENCY CONTACTS

Hospitals

The following hospitals with casualty departments are located in the places shown below. The telephone numbers given are the hospital switchboard; ask to be put through to Accident and Emergency Reception.

◆ Full 24-hour emergency service

▼ Minor injuries only, 24-hour service

▲ Minor injuries only, NOT 24-hour service

Section	Town	Telephone No	Address
1	▲ Devizes	01380 723511	Devizes Hospital, New Park Road, Devizes (daily 8am-10pm)
	▲ Marlborough	01672 514571	Savernake Hospital, London Road, Marlborough (daily 8am-10pm)
	◆ Swindon	01793 604020	The Great Western Hospital, Marlborough Road, Swindon
2	▲ Didcot	01235 205860	Didcot Community Hospital, Wantage Road, Didcot (weekdays 6pm - 8am, weekends/bank hols 24 hrs)
3	▲ Wallingford	01491 208500	Wallingford Community Hospital, Reading Road, Wallingford (daily 9am-5pm)
4	◆ Aylesbury	01296 315000	Stoke Mandeville Hospital, Mandeville Road, Aylesbury

This booklet gives details of the settlements, accommodation, eating places, shops, attractions and other facilities along The Ridgeway. They are listed in geographic order from Overton Hill to Ivinghoe Beacon.

If you fail to find accommodation using this guide please contact the Tourist Information Centres listed near the beginning of each section which may be able to provide other addresses.

The Ridgeway is divided into four sections as indicated on the map on page 5. At the start of each section is a map showing the settlements close to the Trail within that section. These maps are meant only as a guide and you are recommended to use this Companion in conjunction with The Ridgeway National Trail Guide or maps.

You are strongly advised to book accommodation in advance. Whilst booking, do check prices since those quoted here are usually the minimum charged.

For those who would like to enjoy more than a day on The Ridgeway without having to carry all their possessions, many accommodation providers have indicated whether they are willing to transport the luggage you don't need during the day to your next night's accommodation. The fee charged for this service needs to be discussed and agreed at the time of the booking. Accommodation providers have also indicated if they are willing to collect you from The Ridgeway and deliver you back after your stay.

All the information within this Companion is as accurate as possible. Inclusion of accommodation does not constitute a recommendation although it is indicated in the details whether an establishment has a recognised grade awarded to it. If you have any comments or notice any errors, please write to Jos Joslin the National Trails Officer (page 16).

Camping on The Ridgeway

The situation regarding camping on The Ridgeway is, in theory, clear enough; The Ridgeway is privately owned and the public right of way along it is for passage only, not for stopping and camping.

In practice, however, most landowners do not object if a tent is pitched on The Ridgeway for a night and disappears the next morning as long as no litter is left, no damage done, nor camp fires lit. Do not camp in adjoining fields, woods or gallops without prior permission from the landowner.

XII ACCOMMODATION, FACILITIES & SERVICES

Key to Symbols for Settlements

Any comments relate to preceding icon.

map grid reference (see start of each section for relevant maps)

shortest walking distance from The Ridgeway

most convenient train station

telephone

toilets

&WC toilets adapted for disabled users

Tourist Information Centre

pub (usually open lunchtimes 11am-3pm then evenings 6pm-11pm)

bar meals in pub

post office (usual opening hours 9am-5.30pm weekdays; 9:00-12.30pm Sat)

general store (usual opening hours daily 9am-5.30pm Mon-Sat)

cafe/tea shop

restaurant

food take-away

opening hours of services relate to the preceding symbol

S M T W T F S

eg: open all day   closed all day

Post offices, general stores,   Post offices, general stores,
cafe/tea shops - open morning;   cafe/tea shops - open afternoon;
Pubs, bar meals, restaurants,   Pubs, bar meals, restaurants,
takeaways - open lunchtime   takeaways - open evening

£   bank (usually open daily 9.30am-4.30pm Mon-Fri)

cash machine available including outside bank opening hours

☆   tourist attraction

Key to Symbols for Accommodation

Type of accommodation (symbols in margins)

▲ yha   youth hostel   INN   inn

Å   camping   ∪   horse accommodation

[H]   hotel

(See overleaf for key to further accommodation symbols)

Tom Brown's School Museum, Uffington

XII ACCOMMODATION, FACILITIES & SERVICES

The number and price following the symbols for rooms gives the number and price of that type of room available. The same applies to tent/caravan pitches and stabling/grazing for horses. Prices quoted for rooms are the minimum price per room per night for bed and breakfast. The price for single occupancy of double, twin or family rooms is given in brackets eg (£22.00).

Accommodation symbols - hotels, inns, guest houses, B&Bs and youth hostels

	double room		secure cycle storage
	twin room	DRY	clothes/boots drying facilities
	family room		laundry facilities
	single room		transport to and from Trail by arrangement
	no smoking in bedrooms		luggage transported to next overnight stop by arrangement
	children welcome		
	wheelchair access		credit card(s) accepted
	dogs allowed by arrangement	◆	VisitBritain accommodation standard for B&Bs, guest houses, inns
V	caters for vegetarians		
	packed lunches available	★	VisitBritain accommodation standard for hotels
	evening meals available at accommodation or locally		
	grazing for horses		special feature/comment
	stabling for horses		

Accommodation symbols - camping and caravan sites

	tent pitches		showers
	caravan pitches		public telephone
	cold water		laundry facilities
	hot water		site shop
	toilets	CG	camping gas
WC	toilets adapted for disabled users		special feature/comment

28

Section 1

Overton Hill to Uffington Castle

Probably the most remote section of The Ridgeway, this
35 km (22 miles) stretch of broad track runs along the
ridge of chalk downland in Wiltshire and Oxfordshire.
It passes through an immensely rich area of archaeology and
past the only pub directly on the western half of the Trail!

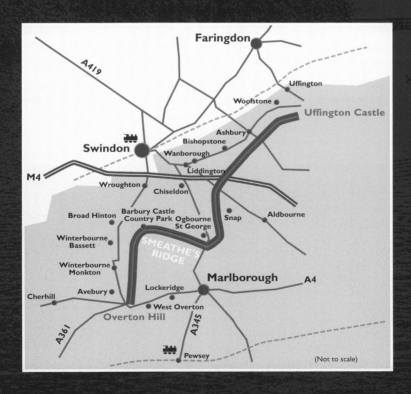

(Not to scale)

A Taster

In places you can feel on top of the world with undulating downland and dry valleys or combes to the south and the Thames Valley stretching away northwards to the Cotswolds in the far distance. A characteristic sight from Overton Hill to Barbury Castle is small clumps of beech woodland planted by the Victorians as landscape features and to give sheep some shelter. Some clumps are even planted on top of Bronze Age round barrows, frowned upon today because of the damage tree roots do to ancient monuments.

The countryside is a mixture of arable land, which changes colour with the seasons, and areas of sheep or cattle grazed grassland. Some of the best views are from Smeathe's Ridge between Barbury Castle and Ogbourne St George.

The villages of Ogbourne St George in the valley of the River Og and those at the foot of the downs such as Bishopstone, Ashbury and Woolstone contain many lovely cottages some of them built out of blocks of chalk with thatched roofs.

This section includes a crossing by bridge of the M4, but the motorway only intrudes upon your journey for a short while and is soon lost as you climb away from it.

Avebury Stone Circle

History

This section starts in what is probably the richest area of archaeology in Britain, the World Heritage Site of Avebury. Within 2 km (1.2 miles) of the start at Overton Hill you can reach the Avebury Stone Circle, Silbury Hill (the largest man-made mound in Europe constructed by Stone Age people using antler picks and shovels made from the shoulder blades of oxen), West Kennett long barrow, the Sanctuary, the Stone Avenue and Fyfield Down National Nature Reserve littered with sarsen stones.

Travelling north, below you at Hackpen Hill you pass the first of the hill figures cut into the chalk which are scattered along the length of The Ridgeway. The Hackpen White Horse was created in 1838 by a local parish clerk. A little further on you reach the first of three Iron Age forts found in this section, Barbury Castle. Unlike the other two, Liddington Castle and Uffington Castle, both of which The Ridgeway skirts, you pass right through the centre of this fort.

Just northeast of Ogbourne St George and to the east of The Ridgeway lies the deserted village of Snap abandoned early this century as a result of agricultural depression. With records dating from 1268, by 1841 Snap was a thriving if small farming community of 47 people. However, cheap corn from America in the 1870s caused the rapid decline in the population and the village's final demise. Today just low piles of sarsen rubble marking the site of cottages remain visible during winter months.

Before you reach Uffington Castle, away to the south is the delightful 17th century Ashdown House set in a tremendous remote dry valley location and the fine Wayland's Smithy long barrow just 50 m north of your route.

Maps		
Landranger maps	173	Swindon and Devizes
	174	Newbury and Wantage
Explorer maps	157	Marlborough and Savernake Forest
	170	Abingdon, Wantage and Vale of White Horse

Public Transport Information

Rail Services   T: 08457 484950 (24 hours a day)
www.nationalrail.co.uk

Bus Services   T: 0870 6082608
www.pti.org.uk

Taxis

Place	Name	Telephone Number
Marlborough	Marlborough Radio Cars	01672 511088
	Arrow Private Hire	01672 515567
Swindon	Swindon Black Cabs	01793 535354/528000
	Link Radio Cars	01793 766666
	Millennium Cars	01793 610000/513333
Lambourn	Ray's	01488 71819

Car Parking

The following are places close to or on The Ridgeway, other than villages or towns, with parking for vehicles - at some only for a few. Unfortunately theft from vehicles parked in the countryside does occasionally occur, so please leave valuables at home.

Place	Map Grid Reference
On Ridgeway at the start at Overton Hill, on north side of A4, 7 km (4.5 miles) west of Marlborough	SU 119681
On Ridgeway at Hackpen Hill on minor road between Marlborough and Broad Hinton, 3 km (2 miles) east of Broad Hinton	SU 129747
On Ridgeway at Barbury Castle Country Park, 8 km (5 miles) south of Swindon signed from Wroughton and Chiseldon	SU 157762

Place	Map Grid Reference
On Ridgeway at Fox Hill near Wanborough, 200m northeast of Shepherds Rest pub on road to Hinton Parva	SU 233814
On Ridgeway 1 km (0.5 miles) south of Ashbury on B4000	SU 274844
National Trust car park for Uffington White Horse, south off B4507, 700m (0.5 miles) north of The Ridgeway	SU 293866

Water Taps

* with troughs for animals

Place	Map Grid Reference
Barbury Castle Country Park (at the café)	SU 158760
Elm Tree Cottage, Southend	SU 198734
• Idstone Barn, Ashbury	SU 263835

Toilets

Place	Map Grid Reference
Barbury Castle Country Park	SU 155762
Shepherds Rest Pub, Fox Hill (patrons only)	SU 232813

Police

Wiltshire	01380 735735
Oxfordshire	08458 505505

Hospitals

Place	Telephone Number	Address
Devizes	01380 723511	Devizes Hospital, New Park Rd, Devizes (daily 8am-10pm)
Marlborough	01672 514571	Savernake Hospital, LondonRd, Marlborough (daily 8am-10pm)
Swindon	01793 604020	The Great Western Hospital, Marlborough Rd, Swindon

Vets

Place	Name	Telephone Number
Marlborough	Holden & Reader	01672 512043
	Hayward & Sercombe	01672 514875
Wroughton	Archway Veterinary Surgery	01793 812542
Swindon	The Drove Veterinary Hospital	01793 522483
	Arrow Veterinary Group	01793 832461
	The Lawn Veterinary Centre	01793 644422
	Thameswood Veterinary Clinic	01793 542300
Lambourn	Hall and Associates	01488 73755
	RGV Valley Equine Hospital	01488 71999
	RGV Valley Pet Clinic	01488 71505
Faringdon	R Elliott	01367 710595
	Christopher Day (Alternative Therapies)	01367 710234

Farriers

Place	Name	Telephone Number
Marlborough	J Baker	01672 514013
Aldbourne	Racing Farriers	01672 540812
Swindon	P J Groom	01793 644123
Wroughton	P A Groom	01793 814185
Lambourn	Chapel Forge Farriers	01488 72613

Saddlers

Place	Name	Telephone Number
Marlborough	G & S Saddlery	01672 515665
Highworth	The Saddlery	01793 766660
Lambourn	Wicks	01488 71766
Faringdon	S and J M Cooper	01367 240517
	The Saddle House	01367 244164

Riding Stables for Guided Rides

Place	Name	Telephone Number
Marlborough	Pewsey Vale Riding Centre	01672 851400

Bike Repairs

Place	Name	Telephone Number
Devizes	Peddlers	01308 722236
Swindon	Mitchell Cycles	01793 523306
	Swindon Cycles	01793 700105
	Bike Doctor	01793 874873
	Total Bike	01793 644185

Mountain Bike Hire

Place	Name	Telephone Number
Devizes	Peddlers (local delivery)	01308 722236
Swindon	Swindon Cycles (local delivery and car rack hire)	01793 700105

Cyclist on Smeathe's Ridge

Tourist Information Centres

★ offers accommodation booking service

Place	Address/Opening Hours
Avebury	Avebury Chapel Centre, Green Street, Avebury SN8 1RE **T**: 01672 539425 **F**: 01672 539296 Opening hours: Summer (1 Apr-31 Oct) Tues-Sun 10:00-17:00 Winter (1 Nov-31 Mar) Thurs-Sun 10:00-17:00
★ Swindon	37 Regent Street, Swindon SN1 1JL **T**: 01793 530328 **F**: 01793 434031 **E**: infocentre@swindon.gov.uk Opening hours: All year: Mon-Sat 09:15-17:00
★ Faringdon	7a Market Place, Faringdon SN7 7HL **T/F**: 01367 242191 Opening hours: Summer (1 Apr-31 Oct) Mon-Fri 10:00-17:00, Sat 10:00-13:00 Winter (1 Nov-31 Mar) Mon-Sat 10:00-13:00

The Royal Oak, Bishopstone

MARLBOROUGH

 SU1969 🥾 **7km (4.4miles)**
🚂 **Swindon 18km (11miles)**
Market town with full range of services

Browns Farm Bed & Breakfast
⚜ GR SU198678 1.5km(0.9miles)
south of Marlborough
Mrs Hazel J Crockford
Browns Farm, Marlborough SN8 4ND
T: 01672 515129 **F:** 01672 515129
E: crockford@farming.co.uk
www.smoothhound.co.uk/hotels/brownsfarmbb.html
🛏 2 £34 🛏 1 £34 🛏 1 £50 (£20)
🚭 ✝ 🐾 V 🏕 🚲 **DRY** **VISA**
Mastercard, Visa, Delta
Ⓢ 2 £10 Ⓦ 2 £10

LOCKERIDGE

 SU1467 🥾 **2.5km (1.6miles)**
🚂 **Swindon 23.5km (14.6miles)**
📞

The Taffrail   *closed Nov - Jan*
Mrs Julia Spencer
Back Lane, Lockeridge, Marlborough
SN8 4ED
T: 01672 861266 **F:** 01672 861266
E: spencer_taffrail@onetel.net.uk
🛏 1 £35 🛏 1 £35 (£20) 🛏 1 £20
🚭 ✝ (over 8 years) V 🚲 **DRY** ⊙
🚗 🏃

Browns Farm

Marlborough, Wilts
Tel 01672 515129
**Peaceful farmhouse set on the edge of
Savernake Forest.**

Tea/coffee facilities, some with en-suite
facilities. Ideal base for touring Wiltshire.
Immediate access to footpaths &
bridleways. Working Dairy/Arable Farm.
TV Lounge and large gardens available
for guests. Ample off-street parking

WEST OVERTON

 SU1367 1km (0.6miles)

🚂 **Swindon 21km (13miles)** 📞

🍺 ⬜⬜⬜⬜⬜⬜⬜⬜⬜
S M T W T F S ✗ ⬜⬜⬜⬜⬜⬜⬜⬜⬜
S M T W T F S

Cairncot

Mrs Rachel Leigh
West Overton, Marlborough SN8 4ER
T: 01672 861617 **M:** 07798 603455
www.cairncot.co.uk

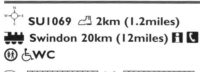 1 £44 (£30) 1 £22 🚭 ♿ ☎ V

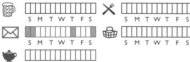 ♦♦♦

🐴 Horse accommodation can be
arranged with neighbour

AVEBURY

 **SU1069** 2km (1.2miles)

🚂 **Swindon 20km (12miles)** 🅿 📞
♿WC

🍺 ⬜⬜⬜⬜⬜⬜⬜⬜⬜
S M T W T F S ✗ ⬜⬜⬜⬜⬜⬜⬜⬜⬜
S M T W T F S

✉ ⬛⬜⬜⬜⬜⬜⬜⬜⬜
S M T W T F S 🛒 ⬜⬜⬜⬜⬜⬜⬜⬜⬜
S M T W T F S

🍵 ⬜⬜⬜⬜⬜⬜⬜⬜⬜
S M T W T F S

☆ Avebury World Heritage Site
T: 01672 539250
www.nationaltrust.org.uk

☆ Alexander Keiller Museum
T: 01672 539250

Manor Farm   *closed Xmas & Easter*

Judith Farthing
Avebury, Marlborough SN8 1RF
T: 01672 539294 **F:** 01672 539294

 1 £65 1 £65 (£45) 🚭 ♿
(over 12 years) V 🏍 🚲 ♦♦♦♦
♿WC

WINTERBOURNE MONKTON

 **SU1072** 3km (1.9miles)

🚂 **Swindon 15km (9miles)** 📞

🍺 ⬜⬜⬜⬜⬜⬜⬜⬜⬜
S M T W T F S ✗ ⬛⬜⬜⬜⬜⬜⬜⬜⬜
S M T W T F S

WINTERBOURNE BASSETT

 **SU1075** 3km (1.9miles)

🚂 **Swindon 13km (8miles)** 📞

🍺 ⬜⬜⬜⬜⬜⬜⬜⬜⬜
S M T W T F S ✗ ⬜⬜⬜⬜⬜⬜⬜⬜⬜
S M T W T F S

BROAD HINTON

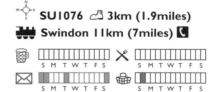 **SU1076** 3km (1.9miles)

🚂 **Swindon 11km (7miles)** 📞

🍺 ⬜⬜⬜⬜⬜⬜⬜⬜⬜
S M T W T F S ✗ ⬜⬜⬜⬜⬜⬜⬜⬜⬜
S M T W T F S

✉ ⬜⬜⬜⬜⬜⬜⬜⬜⬜
S M T W T F S 🛒 ⬛⬜⬜⬜⬜⬜⬜⬜⬜
S M T W T F S

The Avenue, Avebury

Strip Lynchet, Bishopstone

Villiers Inn

Wroughton, Oxfordshire

Tel: 01793 814744   Fax: 01793 814119

★★★ Visit Britain Grade

In 1870 Moormead Farm always ensured that its residents were comfortable, well fed and watered.

Nowadays it is Villiers Inn and the objectives remain the same. Villiers Inn aims to provide exceptional value for money whilst avoiding the dreary monotony that is so typical of the economy hotel genre.

Instead Villiers Inn is a warm-hearted, full-service hotel with personality!

BARBURY CASTLE

SU1476 👞 on path

🚂 Swindon 10km (6miles) (♿)

☆ Barbury Castle Country Park
T: 01793 771419

WROUGHTON

SU1480 👞 4km (2.5miles)

🚂 Swindon 5km (3miles) 📞

&WC

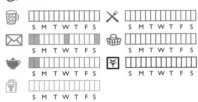

£ Inside Coventry Newsagent
☆ Science Museum
T: 01793 846200
www.sciencemuseum.org.uk/wroughton/

ℍ **Villiers Inn**

The Manager
Moormead Road, Wroughton, Swindon
SN4 9BY
T: 01793 814744 **F:** 01793 814119
E: wroughton@villiershotels.com
www.villiershotels.com/wroughton
🛏 18 £69 11 £69 (£55) 4
£55 🎱 ♿ 📺 V 🍺 🚭 🚲 DRY 🚗
🚶 VISA Mastercard, Visa, American
Express, Delta ★★★

SWINDON

SU1583 👞 9km (5.6miles)

🚂 🛈

Large town with full range of services

☆ STEAM - Museum of the Great
Western Railway
T: 01793 466646
www.steam-museum.org.uk

☆ Swindon Community Heritage
Museum & Art Gallery
T: 01793 466556

☆ Coate Water & Lydiard Country
Parks **T:** 01793 490150

CHISELDON

SU1879 👞 3km (1.9miles)

🚂 Swindon 8km (5miles) 📞

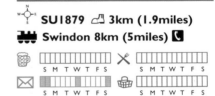

OGBOURNE ST GEORGE

SU2074 🏠 Ikm (0.6miles)

🚌 Swindon 13km (8miles) 📞

🍺 ☐☐☐☐☐☐☐☐ ✕ ☐☐☐☐☐☐☐
    S M T W T F S   S M T W T F S

∪ 𝕏 Foxlynch

Mr George Edwins
Ogbourne St George,
Marlborough SN8 ITD
T: 01672 841307

🛏 I £20/person 👫 💺 🚵 🚲 DRY
🚗 👟

🏕 6 £5/person 🚐 2 £5/person 🚰
🚰 ⚿ 🍽 💺 DRY

☾ 4 £10

∪ Ⓗ Parklands Hotel & Bentleys Restaurant

Mr Mark Bentley
High Street, Ogbourne St George,
Marlborough SN8 ISL
T: 01672 841555 **F:** 01672 841533
E: enquiries@parklandshoteluk.co.uk
www.parklandshoteluk.co.uk

🛏 6 £70 🛏 3 £70 (£65) 🛏 2 £50

🚭 👫 ♿ 💺 V 🚵 🌑 🚲 DRY 👣 VISA

Mastercard, Visa, Delta, Switch, Solo, JCB

◆◆◆◆

☾ 2 £10

LIDDINGTON

⊕ **SU2081** 👢 **1km (0.6miles)**

🚂 **Swindon 7km (4miles)** 📞

🍺 |||||||||| ✕ |||||||||||
    S M T W T F S   S M T W T F S

☆ Liddington Castle

www.themodernantiquarian.com/site/3080

Street House Farm   *closed Xmas*

Mrs Elizabeth Dixon

Liddington, Swindon SN4 0HD

T: 01793 790243

🛏 1 £42 🛏 1 £42 (£25) 🚭 ✲ 🐾

V 🏞 🚲 **DRY** 🔲 🐾

WANBOROUGH

⊕ **SU2182** 👢 **2km (1.2miles)**

🚂 **Swindon 7km (4miles)** 📞

🍺 |||||||||| ✕ |||||||||||
    S M T W T F S   S M T W T F S

📩 |||||||||||
    S M T W T F S

Iris Cottage   *closed Xmas*

Mrs J Rosier

Burycroft, Lower Wanborough, Swindon SN4 0AP

T: 01793 790591

🛏 1 £40 🛏 2 £22 🚭 🏞 🚲 **DRY**

🚗 🐾

Hackpen Hill, Wiltshire

BISHOPSTONE

 SU2483 **1km (0.6miles)**

Swindon 11km (7miles)

S M T W T F S   S M T W T F S

Cheney Thatch

Bishopstone, Swindon,
Wiltshire
Tel 01793 790508

16th Century stone thatched cottage
in unique peaceful setting.
Trout stream through garden,
summer marquee. Heated outdoor
swimming pool. Footpath to
Ridgeway from garden gate.

Cheney Thatch *closed Xmas*

Mrs Rosemary Boot
Oxon Place, Bishopstone,
Swindon SN6 8PS
T: 01793 790508
2 £45 (£30) V DRY
◆◆◆

Prebendal Farm *closed Xmas & New Year*

Mrs Joanna Selbourne
Bishopstone, Swindon SN6 8PT
T: 01793 790485 **F:** 01793 791487
E: prebendal@aol.com
www.prebendal.com
3 £60 1 £60 (£35)
V DRY

The Royal Oak

Mr Brian Walkley
Cues Lane, Bishopstone,
Swindon SN6 8PP
T: 01793 790481 **M:** 07949 010238
F: 01793 790481
E: royaloak_bishopstone@lineone.net
www.royaloak-bishopstone.co.uk
1 £50 1 £50 1
£25/person (£25) V
Mastercard, Visa,
Delta, other

Ashbury

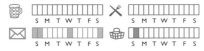

SU2685 🥾 1km (0.6miles)

🚂 Swindon 13km (8miles) 📞

🍺 ||||||||||| ✕ |||||||||||
   S M T W T F S   S M T W T F S

✉ ||||||||||| 🍴 |||||||||||
   S M T W T F S   S M T W T F S

☆ Ashdown House
T: 01488 72584
www.nationaltrust.org.uk

Woolstone

SU2987 🥾 2km (1.2miles)

🚂 Swindon 18km (11miles) 📞

🍺 ||||||||||| ✕ |||||||||||
   S M T W T F S   S M T W T F S

Hickory House *closed Xmas & New Year*

Mrs Caroline Grist
Woolstone, Faringdon SN7 7QL
T: 01367 820303
E: rlg@hickoryhouse.freeserve.co.uk
www.stilwell.co.uk
🛏 2 £48 (£26) 🚫 👪 (over 12 years)
V 🖊 🚲 DRY 🅾 🚗 🚶

Hickory House

Hickory House, Woolstone, Oxfordshire
Tel: 01367 820303

Situated in a delightful village just beneath the White Horse Hill and Uffington Castle, Hickory House offers comfortable accommodation in a self-contained part of the house overlooking a pretty garden and with fine views.

UFFINGTON

 SU3089 🏠 **3km (1.9miles)**

🚂 **Swindon 19km (12miles)** 📞

🍺 |||||||||||||| ✗ ||||||||||||||
  S M T W T F S   S M T W T F S

✉ |||||||||| 🍴 ||||||||||||||
  S M T W T F S   S M T W T F S

🍵 ||||||||||
  S M T W T F S

☆ Tom Brown's School Museum
T: 01367 820259

🔆 GR SU307872 1km(0.6miles) from Ridgeway

Mrs M E A Seymour

Britchcombe Farm, Uffington, Faringdon SN7 7QJ

T: 01367 820667 **M:** 07748 005362

F: 01367 821022

E: marcella@seymour8227freeserve.co.uk

Mobile homes from £120/week

🚭 🏃 🛏 🚿 DRY 📷 🚶

🏕 30 £3/person 🚐 20 £3/person 🚰
🚰 📱 🛗 🛏 DRY 📷

Norton House   *closed Xmas*

Mrs F Oberman

Broad Street, Uffington,
Faringdon SN7 7RA

T: 01367 820230 **F:** 01367 820230

E: carloberman@aol.com

🛏 1 £44 🚿 1 £74 (£30) 🛏 1 £25

🚭 🏃 🛏 V 🛗 🚲 DRY 📷 🚗 🚶

◆◆◆

Sower Hill Farm

🔆 GR SU303876 1.5km(0.9miles)
from Ridgeway

Mrs Sylvia Cox

Uffington, Faringdon SN7 7QH

T: 01367 820758

🛏 1 £45 🚿 1 £45 (£25) 🛏 1 £25

🚭 🏃 (over 12 years) V 🛗 🚲 DRY
🚶

FARINGDON

 SU2895 🏠 **9.5km (6miles)**

🚂 **Swindon 18km (11miles)** 📶

Market town with full range of services

Sudbury House Hotel

Mr Andrew Ibbotson

Folly Hill, Faringdon SN7 8AA

T: 01367 241272 **F:** 01367 242346

E: stay@sudburyhouse.co.uk

www.sudburyhouse.co.uk

🛏 39 £75 🚿 10 £75 🛏 2 £95
(£75) 🏃 ♿ 🛏 V 🛗 🍴 🚲 DRY 📷
🚗 🚶 💳 Mastercard, Visa,
American Express, Delta, Diners

★★★

Section 2

Uffington Castle to Streatley

This 33 km (21 miles) stretch of The Ridgeway keeps to the high scarp edge of the open downland in Oxfordshire and Berkshire and includes the widest parts of the Trail and some of the best conditions underfoot. There's also lots of history to explore.

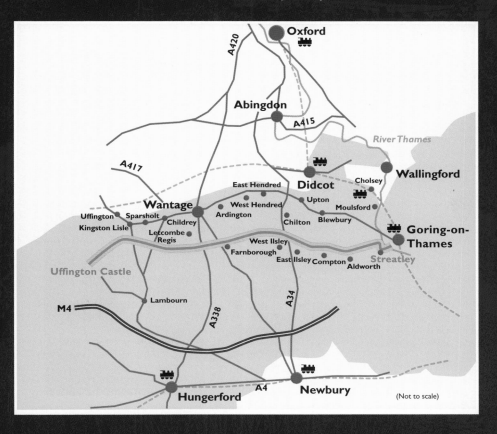

Oxford

A420

Abingdon

A415

River Thames

A417

Wallingford

East Hendred

Didcot

Cholsey

Wantage

Upton

Moulsford

Uffington

Sparsholt

West Hendred

Ardington

Chilton

Blewbury

Kingston Lisle

Childrey

Letcombe Regis

Goring-on-Thames

West Ilsley

Farnborough

East Ilsley

Compton

Aldworth

Streatley

Uffington Castle

Lambourn

A338

A34

M4

Hungerford

A4

Newbury

(Not to scale)

A Taster

Rolling open downland to the south, punctuated in places by small woodlands, and fine views north into the Vale of White Horse and the Thames Valley are typical of this section. On a clear day you can see the hills in the distance behind which nestles Oxford and, further east, the Chiltern Hills through which The Ridgeway later travels. Dominating the view from many places are the cooling towers of Didcot power station just 10 km (6 miles) north, sometimes menacing and inappropriate but at other times strangely beautiful.

This is horse racing country and an early riser will encounter strings of racehorses exercising on the numerous gallops, long ribbons of well managed grass tracks, adjacent to The Ridgeway. The turf of the downland drains easily through the chalk just below creating excellent going for horses.

Small villages are strung out below to the north at the spring line where water seeps between different geological layers. Many of these are worth a visit to enjoy the local vernacular architecture which includes cottages built from chalk blocks quarried from the downs.

This section also negotiates the A34 north-south trunk road by an underpass. The noise of the traffic is counteracted to some extent by the colourful mural depicting local historical scenes painted by local people on the walls of the underpass.

Racehorses on gallops at Kingston Lisle

History

This section is steeped in history from prehistoric times right through to this century. The earliest monuments are the round barrows, burial chambers dating from Bronze Age times, roughly from 2000 to 750 BC. There are several close to The Ridgeway, including one in the area of woodland at Scutchamer's Knob above East Hendred which was excavated and ruthlessly dug away in 1842. Another lies within the width of the path a kilometre west of the B4494 road.

Two Iron Age forts grace this part of The Ridgeway, Uffington Castle and Segsbury Camp. Just a short distance from the former lies the most famous hill figure in the country, the Uffington White Horse, and below this Dragon Hill, a natural mound where, reputedly, St George killed his dragon. The bare chalk patch on the top is said to be where the blood of the dragon was spilt and no grass will now grow.

The Saxons have left their mark in this area with Wantage being the birth place of King Alfred who subsequently fought battles on the downs. Wantage also gave its name to Lord Wantage whose wife erected the monument to her husband on The Ridgeway just east of the B4494. His descendants still own the model farm and villages he built at the end of the last century.

A little further east of here and to the south lies the village of East Ilsley famous for its sheep fairs which only finished in the 1930s.

Statue of King Alfred in Wantage Market Place

Maps

Landranger maps	174	Newbury and Wantage
Explorer maps	170	Abingdon, Wantage and Vale of White Horse

Public Transport Information

Rail Services	08457 484950 (24 hours a day)
	www.nationalrail.co.uk
Bus Services	0870 6082608
	www.pti.org.uk

Taxis

Place	Name	Telephone Number
Lambourn	Ray's	01488 71819
Denchworth	Sapphire Cabs	0800 037 3333
Wantage	Gemini Cars	0800 0282219
	Stuart's Taxis	01235 770608
Grove	Grove Cabs	01235 772200
	Evenload Taxis	01235 762035
East Hendred	Rural Car Services	0800 0743494
Chilton	Rural Carriages	01235 834469
Compton	Compton Passenger Service	01635 579076
Blewbury	Rural Connections	01235 851010
Didcot	Bob's	01235 512121
	Harold's Taxis	01235 512345
	Loder	01235 814679
	Pryor's	01235 812345
	Zodiac Cars	07074 201747
Goring-on-Thames	Murdock's Taxis	01491 875875/872029
	Applecars	01491 874401

Car Parking

The following are places close to or on The Ridgeway, other than villages or towns, with parking for vehicles - at some only for a few. Unfortunately theft from vehicles parked in the countryside does occasionally occur so please leave valuables at home.

Place	Map Grid Reference
National Trust car park for Uffington White Horse, south off B4507, 700m (0.5 miles) north of The Ridgeway	SU 293866
On Ridgeway at Sparsholt Firs on the south side of the B4001, 4km (2.5 miles) south of Childrey	SU 344851
On Ridgeway on the east side of B4494, 5km (3 miles) south of Wantage	SU 417843
On Ridgeway at Scutchamer's Knob, 3km (2 miles) south of E Hendred off the A417 east of Wantage	SU 458851
On Ridgeway at Bury Down on minor road from A34 to W Ilsley (signed Ridgeway from A34)	SU 479841
On Ridgeway at end of Rectory Road, Streatley west off A417	SU 567813

Wantage Monument south of Ardington

Water Taps

- with troughs for animals

Place	Map Grid Reference
• Hill Barn Sparsholt	SU 338854
The Ridgeway Youth Hostel, Letcombe Regis	SU 393849
• Compton Down	SU 506823

Toilets

The Ridgeway Youth Hostel, Letcombe Regis	SU 393849

Police

Oxfordshire and Berkshire	08458 505505

Hospitals

Place	Telephone Number	Name
Swindon	01793 604020	The Great Western Hospital, Marlborough Rd, Swindon
Didcot	01235 205860	Didcot Community Hospital, Wantage Road, Didcot.
	(weekdays 6pm - 8am, weekends/bank holidays 24 hours)	

Vets

Place	Name	Telephone Number
Lambourn	Hall and Associates	01488 73755
	RGV Valley Equine Hospital	01488 71999
	RGV Valley Pet Clinic	01488 71505
Faringdon	R Elliott	01367 710595
	Christopher Day (Alternative Therapies)	01367 710234
Wantage	Abivale Veterinary Group	01235 770333
	Danetree Veterinary Surgery	01235 770227
West Ilsley	The Cottages Veterinary Surgery	01635 281344
Kingston Lisle	Companion Care Veterinary Surgery	01367 820820

Place	Name	Telephone Number
Didcot	Abivale Veterinary Group	01235 511553
	Larkmead Veterinary Group	01235 814991
	Hadden Hill Veterinary Centre	01235 511553
Cholsey	Larkmead Veterinary Group	01491 651479

Farriers

Place	Name	Telephone Number
Lambourn	Chapel Forge Farriers	01488 72613
West Ilsley	A A Weston	01635 281878

Saddlers

Place	Name	Telephone Number
Lambourn	Wicks	01488 71766
Faringdon	S and J M Cooper	01367 240517
	The Saddle House	01367 244164
Goosey (near Faringdon)	Asti Equestrian	01367 710288
Denchworth (near Wantage)	Denchworth Equestrian Supplies	01235 868175
Blewbury	Arena Saddlery	01235 850725

Riding Stables for Guided Rides

Place	Name	Telephone Number
Kingston Lisle	Holistic Horses	01235 821520
Blewbury	Blewbury Riding Centre	01235 851016

Bike Repairs

Place	Name	Telephone Number
Wantage	Ridgeway Cycles	01235 764445
	GMC	01235 764204
Didcot	Dentons	01235 816566
Abingdon	Pedal Power	01235 525123
	Behind Bars	01235 535624

Mountain Bike Hire

Place	Name	Telephone Number
Abingdon	Pedal Power	01235 525123

Tourist Information Centres

★ offers accommodation booking service

Place	Address/Opening Hours
★ Faringdon	7a Market Place, Faringdon SN7 7HL **T/F**: 01367 242191 Opening hours: Summer (1 Apr-31 Oct) Mon-Fri 10:00-17:00, Sat 10:00-13:00 Winter (1 Nov-31 Mar) Mon-Sat 10:00-13:00
★ Wantage	19 Church Street, Wantage OX12 8BL **T/F**: 01235 760176 Opening hours: All year: Mon-Sat 10:30-16:30, Sun 14:30-17.00
★ Abingdon	25 Bridge Street, Abingdon OX14 3HN **T**: 01235 522711 **F**: 01235 535245 Opening hours: Summer (1 Apr-31 Oct) Mon-Sat 10:00-17:00 Sun 13:30-16:15 Winter (1 Nov-31 Mar) Mon-Fri 10:00-16:00, Sat 09:30-14:30
★ Didcot	118 The Broadway, Didcot OX11 8AB **T/F**: 01235 813243 Opening hours: Summer (Jul-Aug) Mon-Sat 10:00-17:00, Sun 10:00-16:00 Winter (Sep-Jun) Mon-Sat 10:00-16:00

Riders on The Ridgeway above Wantage

KINGSTON LISLE

⊕ **SU3287** 👢 **2km (1.2miles)**

🚂 **Swindon 22km (14miles)** 📞

🍺 |||||||||||| ✕ ||||||||||||
    S M T W T F S   S M T W T F S

SPARSHOLT

⊕ **SU3487** 👢 **3km (1.9miles)**

🚂 **Didcot 20km (12miles)** 📞

🍺 |||||||||||| ✕ ||||||||||||
    S M T W T F S   S M T W T F S

Down Barn Farm   *closed Xmas* 🏕⏾

⌖ GR SU333852 600m south of Ridgeway

Mrs P A Reid

Sparsholt Down, Wantage OX12 9XD

M: 07799 833115

E: pendomeffect@aol.com

🛏 1 £40 🛏 2 £40 (£20) 🚭 🚻 ♿
📺 V 🔥 🌐 🚲 DRY 🗇 🚗 🥾
🏕 4 £5 🚐 2 £10 🚰 🚰 🕛 📱 🔌
DRY 🗇

🍴 Evening meals not available every Sunday

🌙 4 £10 🌙 4 £5

Dragon Hill from Whitehorse Hill

CHILDREY

 **SU3687** ⛄ **4km (2.5miles)**

🚂 **Didcot 18km (11miles)** 📞

LETCOMBE REGIS

 **SU3886** 👢 **2km (1.2miles)**

🚂 **Didcot 16km (10miles)** 📞

9 Croft End

Mrs Joyce Coombs

Letcombe Regis, Wantage OX12 9JJ

T: 01235 763694 **M:** 07770 580656

E: clivecoombs@hotmail.com

🛏 1 £55 🛏 1 £50 (£35) 🚭 🚼 ♿
V 🚲 📷

The Old Vicarage

Mrs G F Barton

Letcombe Regis, Wantage OX12 9JP

T: 01235 765827 **M:** 07970 567825

E: hugh.barton@virgin.net

🛏 2 £55 🛏 1 £55 (£30) 🛏 1 £30
🚭 🚼 V 🚲 DRY 📷 🚗 🚶
◆◆◆◆

YHA Ridgeway Centre *phone ahead* 🔺 U

GR SU393849 600m from Ridgeway

The Manager

Court Hill, Letcombe Regis, Wantage

OX12 9NE

T: 01235 760253 **F:** 01235 768865

E: ridgeway@yha.org.uk

www.yharidgeway.org.uk

Mastercard, Visa, Delta

🏕 many £5.15 🔥 🔥 ♿ 📖 DRY 🐕

🏠 Dormitory/private accommodation
from £13.40/adult

🕐 4 £9

WANTAGE

 **SU4088** ⛄ **4km (2.5miles)**

🚂 **Didcot 13km (8miles)** 🏨

Market town with full range of services

☆ The Vale & Downland Museum
T: 01235 771447
www.wantage.com/museum

B & B In Wantage

Mrs E Turner

50 Foliat Drive, Wantage OX12 7AL

T: 01235 760495 **M:** 07729 014265

E: eleanor@eaturner.freeserve.co.uk

🛏 2 £38 🛏 1 £40 (£24) 🚭 🚼 ♿
V 🚲 DRY 📷 ◆◆◆◆

⊙ **Lockinge Kiln Farm** *closed Jan & Feb*

⌖ GR SU424834 1km(0.6miles) south of Ridgeway

Mrs Stella Cowan

Chain Hill, The Ridgeway, Wantage OX12 8PA

T: 01235 763308 **F:** 01235 763308

E: stellacowan@hotmail.com

www.lockingekiln.co.uk

🛏 1 £44 🛏 2 £44 (£28) 🚭 👫 (over 7 years) V 🐾 🖤 🚲 DRY 🥾

◼ Packed lunches & meals not available Saturday or Sunday

⑤ 2 £10 ⑥ 6 £4

ARDINGTON

 **SU4388** 🥾 **4km (2.5miles)**

🚂 **Didcot 10km (6miles)** 📞

WEST HENDRED

 **SU4488** 🥾 **4km (2.5miles)**

🚂 **Didcot 9km (6miles)** 📞

Lockinge Kiln Farm

The Ridgeway, Wantage, Oxfordshire ~ Tel/Fax: **01235 763308**

Comfortable farmhouse enjoying a quiet country location,
just 1/2 mile south of The Ridgeway. Ideal walking /cycling/horseriding.

EAST HENDRED

⌖ **SU4688** 🏃 **4km (2.5miles)**
🚂 **Didcot 7km (4miles)** 📞

🍺 |||||||||| ✕ ||||||||||
　 S M T W T F S　 S M T W T F S
✉ |||||||||| 🧺 ||||||||||
　 S M T W T F S　 S M T W T F S

☆ Champs Chapel Museum
T: 01235 833466/833481

○ A Monk's Court

Mrs Turnbull

Newbury Road, East Hendred, Wantage
OX12 8LG

T: 01235 833797 **M:** 07710 274653
F: 01235 862554 **E:** udsl@udg.org.uk
www.monkscourt.co.uk

🛏 2 £50 🛏 1 £55 (£30) 🚭 ♿ ♿
📷 V 🖐 🚲 DRY 🔲 🚗 ◆◆◆
Ⓖ 2 £5

Cowdrays

Mrs Margaret Bateman

Cat Street, East Hendred, Wantage
OX12 8JT

T: 01235 833313 **M:** 07799 622003
E: cowdrays@virgin.net

🛏 2 £60 🛏 2 £60 (£30) 🛏 1 £30
🚭 ♿ ♿ 📷 V 🖐 🚲 DRY 🔲 🚗 🥾
◆◆◆

WEST ILSLEY

⌖ **SU4782** 🏃 **2km (1.2miles)**
🚂 **Didcot 11km (7miles)** 📞

🍺 |||||||||| ✕ ||||||||||
　 S M T W T F S　 S M T W T F S

CHILTON

⌖ **SU4986** 🏃 **2km (1.2miles)**
🚂 **Didcot 6km (4miles)** 📞

🍺 |||||||||| ✕ ||||||||||
　 S M T W T F S　 S M T W T F S
🫖 ||||||||||
　 S M T W T F S

EAST ILSLEY

⌖ **SU4981** 🏃 **2km (1.2miles)**
🚂 **Didcot 11km (7miles)** 📞

🍺 |||||||||| ✕ ||||||||||
　 S M T W T F S　 S M T W T F S

The Star Inn　　　*closed Xmas* 🏨

Richard Vellender & Kim Ward

High Street, East Ilsley,
Newbury RG20 7LE

T: 01635 281215 **F:** 01635 281107
E: kimrichstar@aol.com
www.starinnhotel.co.uk

🛏 5 £60 🛏 1 £60 🛏 1 £75 (£50)
🛏 3 £50 ♿ ♿ 📷 V 🖐 🚲 🚗
🥾 VISA Mastercard, Visa, Delta, Switch
◆◆◆◆

🍴 No evening meals on Sunday

The Star Inn

Tel 01635 281215

East Ilsley's oldest inn circa 15th century

Serving the finest real ales from the local area. All bedrooms well appointed and en-suite, beer garden, log fires, satellite TV, tea & coffee, 'trouser press'. Listed in 'The Good Pub Guide' and CAMRA'S 'Room at the Inn'

UPTON

 SU5186 🔲 4km (2.5miles)

🚂 Didcot 5km (3miles) 📞

COMPTON

 SU5280 🔲 2km (1.2miles)

🚂 Goring 9km (6miles) 📞

£ HSBC (Tue & Fri am only)

Compton Swan Hotel

Mr Garry Mitchell
High Street, Compton,
Newbury RG20 6NJ
T: 01635 578269 **F:** 01635 579631
E: garry@comptonswan.freeserve.co.uk
www.smoothhound.co.uk/hotels/comptons

🛏 1 £60 🛏 4 £60 🛏 1 £70 (£50)

🚭 🚏 ♿ 🖼 V 🏔 🌙 🚲 DRY 🚗 🐎

💳 Mastercard, Visa, Delta, Switch
🛁 En-suite showers available

BLEWBURY

 SU5385 🔲 4km (2.5miles)

🚂 Didcot 6km (4miles) 📞

Shop is in petrol station

ALDWORTH

 SU5579 🥾 **2km (1.2miles)**

🚂 **Goring 5km (3miles)** 📞

Fieldview Cottage   *closed Xmas*

Mr & Mrs Bette & Harold Hunt
Bell Lane, Aldworth, Reading RG8 9SB
T: 01635 578964
E: hunt@fieldview.freeserve.co.uk
🛏 1 £60 🛏 1 £60 (£30) 🛏 1 £30
🚭 👫 (over 10 years) & V 🚲 DRY
⬜ ◆◆◆◆

MOULSFORD-ON-THAMES

 SU5983 🥾 **2km (1.2miles)**

🚂 **Cholsey 3km (2miles)** 📞

White House   *closed Xmas & New Year*

Mrs Maria Watsham
Moulsford-on-Thames,
Wallingford OX10 9JD
T: 01491 651397 **F:** 01491 652560
E: mwatsham@tiscali.co.uk
🛏 1 £60 1 £60 (£40) 🛏 1 £35

◆◆◆◆ VisitBritain Silver Award

STREATLEY

 SU5980 🥾 **on path**

🚂 **Goring 1km (0.5miles)** 📞

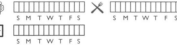

☆ Beale Park
T: 0118 9845172
www.bealepark.co.uk

☆ Basildon Park
T: 0118 9843040
www.nationaltrust.org.uk

Aldworth church

YOUTH HOSTELS
Court Hill, Streatley, Bradenham and Ivinghoe

There are four Youth Hostels - at Court Hill, Streatley, Bradenham and Ivinghoe - along The Ridgeway National Trail, all offering affordable, friendly and comfortable accommodation in family rooms or dormitories. Prices start from £11.80 per night and meals are excellent value at £5.10 for evening and £3.50 for full breakfast. The YHA is a membership organisation; non-members are welcome to join on arrival at any Youth Hostel.

- Court Hill
- Streatley
- Bradenham
- Ivinghoe

Pennyfield B&B *closed Xmas & New Year*

Mrs M A Vanstone
The Coombe, Streatley,
Reading RG8 9QT
T: 01491 872048 **F:** 01491 872048
E: mandrvanstone@hotmail.com
www.pennyfield.co.uk
🛏 2 £55 🛏 1 £55 (£55) ⊗ ♯♦
(over 12 years) V 🐾 🚲 DRY 📷 🚗
♿ ◆◆◆◆ ⊌ VisitBritain Silver Award

YHA Streatley *phone ahead*

The Manager
Hill House, Reading Road, Streatley,
Reading RG8 9JJ
T: 01491 872278 **F:** 01491 873056
E: streatley@yha.org.uk
www.yhastreatley.org.uk
⊗ ♯♦ V 🐾 🚲 DRY
⊌ Dormitory/private accommodation
from £13.40/adult

Red kite, once again common in the Chilterns

St Botolph's, Swyncombe, early Norman church dedicated to the patron saint of travellers

Section 3

Streatley to Chinnor

This 33 km (21 miles) section of The Ridgeway in Oxfordshire is full of variety and charm. It passes through a couple of villages as it follows the River Thames before heading into the more wooded, yet still undulating, Chiltern Hills via an ancient Grim's Ditch and finishes on the wide track of the old Icknield Way.

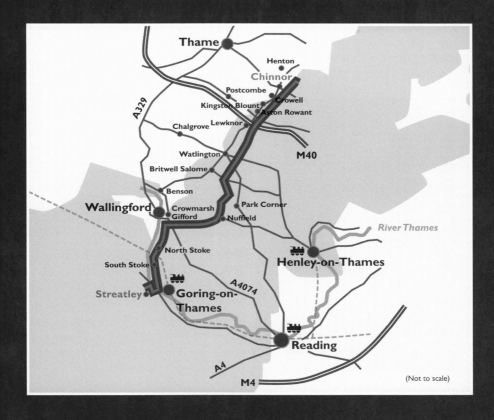

(Not to scale)

A Taster

Water, woodlands and small villages are features of this part of The Ridgeway, contrasting considerably with the open and more remote countryside of Sections One and Two.

England's most famous river, the River Thames, is your companion for the first few kilometres and as you follow it you'll pass through water meadows grazed by cattle and the two lovely villages of South and North Stoke. On the opposite bank, another National Trail runs, The Thames Path which The Ridgeway crossed at Goring bridge. Then as you strike east you'll walk on a narrow secluded path alongside a Grim's Ditch for a considerable distance, much of it surrounded by woodland bright with bluebells and wood anemones during spring.

From the village of Nuffield you turn north and soon reach the small hamlet of Swyncombe, an area which is probably one of the remotest and loveliest parts of the Chilterns. Here, the small flint church of St Botolph's has been beautifully restored.

Descending from Swyncombe to near the base of the scarp, The Ridgeway picks up the Upper Icknield Way and follows this broad track for the remaining 13 km (8 miles) to Chinnor. This latter part can be enjoyed by horseriders and cyclists as well as walkers and during wet times of the year gets muddy in places. The first 8 km (5 miles) of this Icknield Way section can also legally be used by drivers of vehicles.

Agriculture along this section is varied and includes a variety of crops and animal grazing. Many of the woodlands in the area, too, are managed for timber.

A few kilometres before Chinnor you'll cross the M40 by an underpass where the motorway slices through the Aston Rowant Nature Reserve in a deep cutting.

Autumn near Wendover

History

The variety of landscape in this section is also reflected in the history of the area with the National Trail encountering amongst other things four important trading routes; the prehistoric Icknield Way, the River Thames used continuously for trading, the Great Western Railway constructed in the 19th century and, of course, today's motorway. The railway makes its impact unpleasantly felt as you initially walk north from Goring, but further along the Thames your path passes beneath Brunel's splendid bridge built in 1839 with its skewed arches and unusual brickwork - well worth a look.

Grim's Ditch is a fascinating ancient earthwork which accompanies you for several kilometres. It's amazing to think such a ditch was constructed using just antler picks as tools. Before you reach the Icknield Way you walk through several areas of woodland dominated by beech trees, and views of others stay with you to Chinnor.

Most of the beech trees you see today have been planted. From the 17th century the wood has been used, initially to supply a cheap source of fuel and charcoal for London and then in the last century by craftsmen. Tent-peg makers and chair leg turners, the bodgers, flourished throughout the Chilterns with the industry centred on High Wycombe. Few bodgers remain but the woodlands still have a commercial and leisure value.

As you pass Watlington it's worth looking to the south to the hillside rearing above you to spy the Watlington White Mark, another of the chalk figures cut into the hills through which The Ridgeway wanders.

Maps		
Landranger maps	174	Newbury and Wantage
	175	Reading and Windsor
	165	Aylesbury and Leighton Buzzard
Explorer maps	171	Chiltern Hills West

Public Transport Information

Rail Services   08457 484950 (24 hours a day)
                             www.nationalrail.co.uk

Bus Services   0870 6082608
                             www.pti.org.uk

Taxis

Place	Name	Telephone Number
Goring-on-Thames	Murdock's Taxis	01491 875875/872029
	Applecars	01491 874401
Wallingford	Hills Taxis	01491 837022
	Rival Car Services	0800 0743494
Benson	A Cabs	01491 839982
	Pontings Taxis	01491 826679
Ewelme	Bushers Taxis	01491 826161
Henley-on-Thames	Chiltern Taxis	01491 578899/577888
	Talbot Taxi	01491 574222
	1st Select Cars	01491 414444
Nettlebed	David Byers	01491 641159
Thame	Premier Cars	01844 216633/217700
	Thame Taxis	01844 216161/214433/215000
	T & B Chauffeur Service	01844 261116
Chinnor	Chinnor Cabs	01844 353637

Car Parking

The following are places close to or on The Ridgeway, other than villages or towns, with parking for vehicles - at some only for a few. Unfortunately theft from vehicles parked in the countryside does occasionally occur so please leave valuables at home.

Place	Map Grid Reference
Goring-on-Thames public car park	SU 599807
On Ridgeway on west side of minor road, 1.5 km (1 mile) southeast of Britwell Salome	SU 681922
On Ridgeway on east side of Hill Road, minor road to Christmas Common 1 km (0.5 miles) southeast of Watlington	SU 698940
On Ridgeway on east side of minor road to Bledlow Ridge 1 km (0.5 miles) south of Chinnor	SP 761003

Water Taps

- with troughs for animals

Place	Map Grid Reference
Grimsdyke Cottage, Grim's Ditch	SU 660872
Church, Nuffield (on the wall)	SU 667874
• White Mark Farm Camp Site, Watlington (March-October)	SU 697939

Toilets

Place	Map Grid Reference
Goring-on-Thames (Car Park off Station Road)	SU 660872
White Mark Farm Camp Site, Watlington (March-October)	SU 697939
Watlington (High Street)	SU 689945

Police

Oxfordshire   08458 505505

Hospitals

Place	Telephone Number	Address
Wallingford	01491 208500	Wallingford Community Hospital, Reading Road, Wallingford (daily 9am-5pm)

Vets

Place	Name	Telephone Number
Benson	Larkmead Veterinary Group	01491 651479
Wallingford	White and Stewart	01491 839043
Watlington	Crossroads Veterinary Centre	01491 612799
Aston Rowant	R E Baskerville	01844 352090
Chinnor	Sprinz and Nash	01844 212000

Farriers

Place	Name	Telephone Number
Chalgrove	Christopher Selwyn	01865 890581

Saddlers

Place	Name	Telephone Number
Turville	Alice Nuttgens Saddlers	01491 638700

Bike Repairs

Place	Name	Telephone Number
Pangbourne	Mountain High	0118 984 1851
Wallingford	Rides on Air	01491 836289
Thame	Thame Cycles	01844 261520

Mountain Bike Hire

Place	Name	Telephone Number
Wallingford	Rides on Air (summer only - local delivery)	01491 836289

Tourist Information Centres

★ offers accommodation booking service

Place	Address/Opening Hours
★ Wallingford	Town Hall, Market Place, Wallingford OX10 0EG **T**: 01491 826972 **F**: 01491 832925 Opening hours: All year: Mon-Sat 09:30-17:00
★ Thame (★ Visitors to office only)	Market House, North Street, Thame OX9 3HH **T/F**: 01844 212834 Opening hours: All year: Mon-Fri 09:30-17:00, Sat 10:00-16:00

Wormsley Estate, south of The Ridgeway

Brunel's railway bridge over the Thames between South and North Stoke

Looking from Ladies Walk to Jacob's Tent, Swyncombe

GORING-ON-THAMES

⊕ SU6080 🥾 on path
🚉 Goring & Streatley 📞 ♿WC

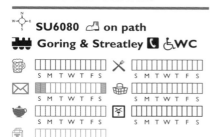

	S M T W T F S		S M T W T F S

£ HSBC 🏧, Lloyds TSB

🏨 Miller of Mansfield

Martin Williamson
High Street, Goring-on-Thames, Reading
RG8 9AW
T: 01491 872829 **F:** 01491 874200
www.millerofmansfield.co.uk
🛏 5 £65 🛏 3 £65 🛏 1 £70 🛏 2
£50 ⛄ ♿ V 🚵 🚫 🚲 DRY 💳
Mastercard, Visa ◆◆◆

Northview House *closed Xmas & New Year*

Mrs I Sheppard
Farm Road, Goring-on-Thames, Reading
RG8 0AA
T: 01491 872184 **E:** hi@goring-on-
thames.freeserve.co.uk
🛏 2 £40 🛏 1 £40 🛏 1 £55 (£25)
🚫 ⛄ ♿ V 🚵 🚲 DRY 🔘 🏃

SOUTH STOKE

⊕ SU5983 🥾 on path
🚉 Goring & Streatley 3km
(2miles) 📞

The Old Post Office

Mrs Vanessa Guiver
The Street, South Stoke, Wallingford
RG8 0JS
T: 01491 871872 **M:** 07889 757767
F: 01491 871873
E: vanessa.guiver@btopenworld.com
🛏 1 £75 (£40) 🚫 V 🚵 🚫 🚲 DRY
🔘 🏃

South Stoke Church

NORTH STOKE

🧭 **SU6086** 👢 **on path**
🚂 **Goring & Streatley 6km (4miles)** 📞

Footpath Cottage

Mrs R G Tanner
The Street, North Stoke,
Wallingford OX10 6BJ
T: 01491 839763
🛏 2 £40 - 45 (£35) 🛏 1 £25 🚭 ⭑
🐾 V 🚲 🌀 🚴 **DRY**
♿ En-suite available

🏨 The Springs Hotel & Golf Club

The Manager
Wallingford Road, North Stoke,
Wallingford OX10 6BE
T: 01491 836687 **F:** 01491 836877
E: info@thespringshotel.com
www.thespringshotel.com
🛏 17 £105 🛏 10 £105 🛏 2 £135
🛏 2 £95 ⭑ 🐾 V 🚲 🌀 🚴 **DRY** 📷
VISA Mastercard, Visa, American Express,
Delta ♿ Non-smoking rooms available

CROWMARSH GIFFORD

🧭 **SU6189** 👢 **1km (0.6miles)**
🚂 **Didcot 10km (6miles)** 📞

Blenheim Farm House *closed Xmas & New Year*

☸ GR SU636882 500m north of
Ridgeway
Mrs Jeny Sarreti
Old Icknield Way,
Wallingford OX10 6PR
T: 01491 832368
E: peter.sarreti@which.net
🛏 1 £50 (£35) 🛏 1 £28 🚭 V 🚲
🚴 **DRY** 🚗 ♿

Bridge Villa Camping & Caravan Park *closed Jan* ⛺

Mr E L Townsend
Crowmarsh Gifford,
Wallingford OX10 8HB
T: 01491 836860 **M:** 07710 452429
F: 01491 836793
⛺ 122 £8 🚐 122 £10 🚿 🚰 ♿WC
📺 📷 CG 🐾 🚴 **VISA** Mastercard,
Visa, Delta

Little Gables B & B

Mr & Mrs A Reeves
166 Crowmarsh Hill,
Wallingford OX10 8BG
T: 01491 837834 **M:** 07860 148882
F: 01491 834426
E: jill@stayingaway.com
www.stayingaway.com
🛏 1 £50 🛏 1 £50 🛏 1 £65 (£35)
🚭 ⭑ V 🚲 🚴 **DRY** ♿ ◆◆◆◆

Little Gables

◆◆◆◆ VisitBritain grade
Tel: 01491 837834

Close to the market town of Wallingford, in the cul-sac road of Crowmarsh Hill on the A4130 between Henley and Oxford. 2 miles from Cholsey station. Easy access to the M4 & M40 Gatwick bus link. Close to Ridgeway and Thames Path and cycle route.

WALLINGFORD

⊹ **SU6089** 🦶 **2km (1.2miles)**
🚋 **Cholsey 9km (6miles)** 🅷
Market town with full range of services

☆ Wallingford Museum
T: 01491 835065
www.galatham.demon.co.uk

52 Blackstone Road
Mrs Enid Barnard
Wallingford OX10 8JL
T: 01491 201917
E: enid.barnard@ntlworld.com
🛏 1 £35 (£23) 🛏 1 £18 🚭 V 🚲
DRY

The George Hotel 🅷
Mr Oliver Round-Turner
High Street, Wallingford OX10 0BS
T: 01491 836665 **F:** 01491 825359
E: info@george-hotel-wallingford.com
www.peelhotel.com
🛏 21 £95 🛏 8 £95 🛏 1 £110
(£85) 🛏 9 £55 🚼 ♿ V 🚳 🚭 🚲 📷
💳 Mastercard, Visa, American Express, Delta, Switch, Solo ★★★ 🅷 Smoking permitted in some rooms only

The Studio
Mrs Pamela Mary Smith
85 Wantage Road,
Wallingford OX10 0LT
T: 01491 837277 **F:** 01491 825036
E: pam@prufit.co.uk www.prufit.co.uk
🛏 1 £50 🛏 1 £50 (£30) 🛏 1 £25
🚭 🚼 (over 4 years) ♿ 📷 V 🚲 **DRY**
🚗

BENSON

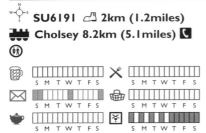

SU6191 🥾 2km (1.2miles)

🚂 Cholsey 8.2km (5.1miles) 📞

♿

| 🍺 | S M T W T F S | ✕ | S M T W T F S |

| ✉ | S M T W T F S | 🧺 | S M T W T F S |

| 🫖 | S M T W T F S | 🍴 | S M T W T F S |

⛽ at BP service station
☆ Veteran Cycles
T: 01491 838414

Fyfield Manor

Mrs Christine Brown
Benson, Wallingford OX10 6HA
T: 01491 835184 **F:** 01491 825635
E: chris@fifield-software.demon.co.uk
www.bedandbreakfastnationwide.com

🛏 1 £55 🛏 1 £55 (£35) 🚭 👫
(over 10 years) **V** 🚲 **DRY** 🚗

◆◆◆◆ 🅷 VisitBritain Silver Award

Grim's Ditch east of Wallingford

NUFFIELD

⊕ **SU6687** 👢 **on path**
🚂 **Henley-on-Thames 11km (7miles)** ☎

  ✕
S M T W T F S   S M T W T F S

☆ Nuffield Place
T: 01491 641224
www.nuffield-place.com

⚑ The Rectory

Mr J Shearer
Nuffield, Henley-on-Thames RG9 5SN
T: 01491 641305 **F:** 01491 641305
🛏 1 £36 🛏 1 £36 🛏 1 £36 (£20)
🛏 1 £20 🚫 ♦♦ V 🔥 🚲 DRY 👢
⚑ 5 £2/person 🚐 1 £5 🔥 🚰
♿ DRY

14 Bradley Road   *closed Xmas*

Miss Diana Chambers
Huntercombe Place, Nuffield, Henley-on-Thames RG9 5SG
T: 01491 641359 **M:** 07747 642056
F: 0118 3738402
E: diana.chambers@rwethameswater.com
🛏 2 £52 🛏 1 £52 (£30) 🚫 ♦♦ 🔲
V 🔥 🚲 DRY ⊙ 🚗 👢
♻ Free transfer to Henley for meals when unavailable in village

PARK CORNER

⊕ **SU6988** 👢 **2km (1.2miles)**
🚂 **Henley-on-Thames 10km (6miles)**

Parkcorner Farm House

Mrs S M Rutter
Park Corner, Nettlebed, Henley-on-Thames RG9 6DX
T: 01491 641450
E: parkcorner_farmhouse@hotmail.com
🛏 2 £50 (£28) 🛏 1 £28 🚫 ♦♦ 🔲 🔥
🚲 DRY 🚗 👢
♻ Free transport to pub

BRITWELL SALOME

⊕ **SU6787** 👢 **1km (0.6miles)**
🚂 **Henley-on-Thames 17km (11miles)** ☎

S M T W T F S   S M T W T F S

Huttons

Mrs J Bowater
Britwell Salome, Watlington OX49 5LH
T: 01491 614389 **M:** 07736 270803
F: 01491 614993
E: jbowater@etonwell.com
🛏 2 £45 🛏 1 £48 (£25) ♦♦ 🔲 V
🔥 🌙 🚲 DRY 🚗 👢
Mastercard, Visa, American Express, Delta ◆◆◆

WATLINGTON

SU6894 🥾 1km (0.6miles)

🚂 Henley 16km (10miles) 📞

♿**WC**

🍺									✕								
	S	M	T	W	T	F	S			S	M	T	W	T	F	S
✉									🧺								
	S	M	T	W	T	F	S			S	M	T	W	T	F	S
☕									🔪								
	S	M	T	W	T	F	S			S	M	T	W	T	F	S
🎁																
	S	M	T	W	T	F	S									

£ Barclays, Link cash machine in Co-Op 🔳

Bowler's Piece

Mrs Penny Cole

16 Couching Street, Watlington OX49 5QQ

T: 01491 614241 **F:** 01491 614345

E: bookings@bowlerspiece.com

www.bowlerspiece.com

🛏 2 £60 🍴 2 £70 🚭 🚻 (over 12 years) **V** 🚶 🚲 🔲 🚗 🐾 💳

Mastercard, Visa, Delta, Switch

⛺ White Mark Farm *closed 31 Oct-1 Mar*

🔧 GR SU698939 50m from Ridgeway

Mrs R J Williams

82 Hill Road, Watlington OX49 5AF

T: 01491 612295

⛺ many £3.50/person 🚐 5 £3.50/person 🚿 🚿 🍳 📗 🔧 🚲 **DRY**

Woodgate Orchard Cottage

Mrs Ronnie Roberts

Howe Road, Watlington OX9 5EL

T: 01491 612675 **F:** 01491 612675

E: mailbox@wochr.freeserve.co.uk

🛏 2 £56 🍴 2 £56 (£30) 🚭 🚻 **V**

🚶 🚲 **DRY** 🚗 🐾 ◆◆◆◆

♿**WC** ☎ Organic food available

CHALGROVE

SU6397 🥾 7km (4.4miles)

🚂 Didcot 20km (12miles) 📞

🍺									✕								
	S	M	T	W	T	F	S			S	M	T	W	T	F	S
✉									🧺								
	S	M	T	W	T	F	S			S	M	T	W	T	F	S

Cornerstones *closed Xmas*

Mrs M A Duxbury

1 Cromwell Close, Chalgrove OX44 7SE

T: 01865 890298 **M:** 07814 543013

E: corner.stones@virgin.net

🍴 2 £40 (£25) 🚭 🚻 (over 5 years) ♿ 🔲 **V** 🚶 🚲 **DRY** 🔲 🚗 🐾 ◆◆◆

Wood anenome

LEWKNOR

 SU7197 ⛰ 1km (0.6miles)

🚂 **Princes Risborough 12km (7miles)** 📞

🍺 ⬚⬚⬚⬚⬚⬚⬚ ✕ ⬚⬚⬚⬚⬚⬚⬚
　 S M T W T F S 　 S M T W T F S

🧺 ⬚⬚⬚⬚⬚⬚⬚
　 S M T W T F S

☆ Cowleaze Wood Sculpture Trail
www.chilternsculpturetrail.co.uk

POSTCOMBE

 SU7099 ⛰ 2.5km (1.6miles)

🚂 **Princes Risborough 13km (8miles)** 📞

🍺 ⬚⬚⬚⬚⬚⬚⬚ ✕ ⬚⬚⬚⬚⬚⬚⬚
　 S M T W T F S 　 S M T W T F S

Beech Farm

Mrs Jackie Graham

Salt Lane, Postcombe, Thame OX9 7EE

T: 01844 281240 **M:** 07973 506443

F: 01844 281632

E: beech.farm@btopenworld.com

www.beechfarm.co.uk

🛏 1 £50 🛏 2 £50 (£35) Ⓢ ♀♂
(over 3 years) ♿ 🔲 V 🚶 🚲 DRY ⬚

🚗 👣 💳 Mastercard, Visa, Switch
◆◆◆◆

ASTON ROWANT

 SU7298 ⛰ 1km (0.6miles)

🚂 **Princes Risborough 10km (6miles)** 📞

🍺 ⬚⬚⬚⬚⬚⬚⬚ ✕ ⬚⬚⬚⬚⬚⬚⬚
　 S M T W T F S 　 S M T W T F S

Peel Guest House

Mrs Sandra Catlin

London Road, Aston Rowant,
Watlington OX49 5SA

T: 01844 351310 **F:** 01844 351310

E: peelguesthouse@btinternet.com

🛏 1 £50 🛏 2 £50 (£35) V 🚲
DRY 🅷 Self-catering accommodation
from £45/night

Tower Cottage

Mrs Margaret Mason

Chinnor Road, Aston Rowant,
Watlington OX49 5SH

T: 01844 354676 **M:** 07721 676150

F: 01844 355999

E: towercottagebb@aol.com www.tower-
cottage.co.uk

🛏 2 £45 🛏 1 £45 🛏 1 £65 (£35)
Ⓢ ♀♂ 🔲 V 🚶 🚲 DRY ⬚ 👣 ◆◆◆

🅷 En-suite available

KINGSTON BLOUNT

⌖ **SU7399** 👢 **0.8km (0.5miles)**

🚂 **Princes Risborough 10km (6miles)** 📞

🍺 |⎺⎺⎺⎺⎺⎺⎺⎺⎺⎺⎺| ✕ |⎺⎺⎺⎺⎺⎺⎺⎺⎺⎺⎺|
S M T W T F S   S M T W T F S

CROWELL

⌖ **SU7499** 👢 **0.8km (0.5miles)**

🚂 **Princes Risborough 9km (5.6miles)**

🍺 |⎺⎺⎺⎺⎺⎺⎺⎺⎺⎺⎺| ✕ |▮⎺⎺⎺⎺⎺⎺⎺⎺⎺⎺|
S M T W T F S   S M T W T F S

CHINNOR

⌖ **SP7500** 👢 **1km (0.6miles)**

🚂 **Princes Risborough 7km (4miles)** 📞 ♿WC

🍺 |⎺⎺⎺⎺⎺⎺⎺⎺⎺⎺⎺| ✕ |⎺⎺⎺⎺⎺⎺⎺⎺⎺⎺⎺|
S M T W T F S   S M T W T F S

✉ |▮▮▮▮▮⎺⎺⎺⎺⎺⎺| 🧺 |⎺⎺⎺⎺⎺⎺⎺⎺⎺⎺⎺|
S M T W T F S   S M T W T F S

🫖 |▮▮▮▮▮⎺⎺⎺⎺⎺⎺| 🗓 |⎺⎺⎺⎺⎺⎺⎺⎺⎺⎺⎺|
S M T W T F S   S M T W T F S

🏧 |⎺⎺⎺⎺⎺⎺⎺⎺⎺⎺⎺|
S M T W T F S

🏦 Royal Bank of Scotland

☆ Chinnor & Princes Risborough Railway

T: 01844 353535

www.cprra.co.uk

Conigre Cottage

Mrs Heidi Clarke

6a Lower Road, Chinnor OX39 4DT

T: 01844 353769 **M:** 07715 931907

F: 01844 353769

🛏 2 £50 (£35) 👢 1 £25 🚻 (over 5 years)  🚺 En-suite available. Small dogs only

HENTON

⌖ **SP7602** 👢 **1.5km (1mile)**

🚂 **Princes Risborough 5km (3miles)** 📞

🍺 |⎺⎺⎺⎺⎺⎺⎺⎺⎺⎺⎺| 🗓 |▮⎺⎺⎺⎺⎺⎺⎺⎺⎺⎺|
S M T W T F S   S M T W T F S

Manor Farm Cottage

Mr & Mrs Trevor & Jean Dixon

Henton, Chinnor OX39 4AE

T: 01844 353301 **M:** 07717 120000

F: 01844 351883

E: dixonhenton@aol.com

www.manorfarmcottage.info

🛏 1 £55 🛏 1 £55 (£38) 🚭 🚻 🔲
V 🚲 DRY 🗓 ♿ ◆◆◆

Section 4

Chinnor to Ivinghoe Beacon

This 37 km (23 miles) eastern stretch of The Ridgeway wanders its way through wonderful wooded parts of the Chiltern Hills before emerging, just a few kilometres from its finish, into more open downland countryside reminiscent of the landscape surrounding its earlier stages. Keeping mainly to quiet footpaths, the Trail skirts around or dips into a few Chiltern settlements where welcome refreshments are easily available.

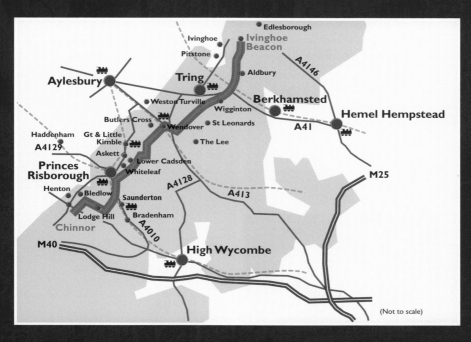

Edlesborough

Ivinghoe

Ivinghoe Beacon

Pitstone

Aldbury

A4146

Aylesbury

Tring

Weston Turville

Wigginton

Berkhamsted

Hemel Hempstead

Butlers Cross

St Leonards

A41

Wendover

Haddenham

Gt & Little Kimble

The Lee

A4129

Askett

M25

Princes Risborough

Lower Cadsden

Whiteleaf

A4128

A413

Henton

Bledlow

Saunderton

Lodge Hill

Bradenham

Chinnor

A4010

M40

High Wycombe

(Not to scale)

A Taster

Dominated by fine beech woodlands for which the Chiltern Hills are justly famous, this countryside however offers more than just trees. Probably the most undulating with several usually reasonably gentle climbs in and out of valleys, this section of The Ridgeway gives some marvellous experiences.

One minute you may be walking up a sheltered slope amongst the tall, straight, grey trunks of beeches and the next you'll have emerged into some fine unimproved chalk grassland boasting a great variety of wild flowers and insects with tremendous views across the Vale of Aylesbury. Or, turning a corner you'll reach the edge of a wood and have a view, framed by branches, of a secluded valley with just a small brick and timber farm complex nestling below you.

Agriculture is varied with crops grown in places, and sheep, cattle and horses grazed elsewhere. Many places are in fact nature reserves where the sheep and cattle are essential elements of the management to ensure the traditional chalk grasslands remain free of scrub and rich in wild species. The woodlands, too, are not just places for leisure as many are managed commercially for their timber.

You pass close to Princes Risborough and through the centre of Wendover, both typical and attractive small Chilterns towns, as well as going near some lovely villages. On Coombe Hill, marked by its monument, you will find yourself at the highest point of the Chiltern Hills with views on a clear day, extending as far as the Berkshire Downs and the Cotswolds. Just beyond Tring you reach the busy A41 trunk road but you cross it high above on a bridge specially built to carry The Ridgeway and it's soon forgotten.

North of Tring Station

History

There's plenty of historical interest to explore close to the route you follow in this section.

For those interested in prehistoric sites, there are long and round barrows, Iron Age forts, and sections of Grim's Ditch to seek out. The oldest barrow, a New Stone Age long barrow at least 4000 years old, is located on Whitelaf Hill just a stone's throw from the Cross cut in the chalk of the north facing slope. For those skilled at finding them, Bronze Age round barrows dating roughly from 2000 to 750 BC, exist in many places with the most obvious situated just to the north of the path at the bottom of the slope up to Ivinghoe Beacon.

And once you reach your journey's end at the top of Beacon Hill itself, there's an Iron Age fort to greet you. Earlier you will have skirted the edge of a similar fort on Pulpit Hill north of the small village of Lower Cadsden. On Pitstone Hill as you emerge from the woodland of Aldbury Nowers, you walk for a while on the edge of a section of Grim's Ditch. This one, unlike that in section 3, is in the open surrounded by chalk grassland.

There is also ample evidence of Man's more recent activities. There are chalk figures cut into the side of the hills at Bledlow and Whitelaf, a memorial to the men of Buckinghamshire who died during the Boer War in South Africa at the turn of this century atop the highest point in the Chilterns, Coombe Hill, and two important country houses, Chequers, the Prime Minister's country residence, and Tring Park close to the Trail.

Maps

Landranger maps	165	Aylesbury and Leighton Buzzard
Explorer maps	181	Chiltern Hills North

Public Transport Information

Rail Services   08457 484950 (24 hours a day)
www.railtrack.co.uk

Bus Services   0870 6082608
www.pti.org.uk

Taxis

Place	Name	Telephone Number
Chinnor	Chinnor Cabs	01844 353637
Princes Risborough	Executive Hire	01844 273733
	B&V Taxis	01844 342079
Aylesbury	Arrowtax	0800 0277698
	Regal Cars	01296 398528
	Butlers	01296 583577
	J Cars	01296 338811
High Wycombe	Atlas Cars & Minibuses	01494 535393
	Ken Banford	01494 441571
	Neale's Taxis	01494 463399
	Arrow Cars	01494 473717
Wigginton	Diamond Cars	01442 890303
	Jaytax	01494 786033
	Town & Country Cabs	01442 875757
Tring	A1 John Taxis	01442 828828/828848
	Bev's Cars	01442 824105/890003
	Mike's Private Hire	01442 826161
Dunstable	A S Glider	01582 666611/602020

Car Parking

The following are places close to or on The Ridgeway, other than villages or towns, with parking for vehicles - at some only for a few. Unfortunately theft from vehicles parked in the countryside does occasionally occur so please leave valuables at home.

Place	Map Grid Reference
On Ridgeway on east side of minor road to Bledlow Ridge 1 km (0.5 miles) south of Chinnor	SP 761003
Princes Risborough public car park	SP 810034
Whiteleaf car park, 1 km (0.5 miles) east of Princes Risborough. Turn right off A4010 at Monks Risborough and car park is on left at top of escarpment	SP 824036
National Trust car park for Coombe Hill, 2 km (1 mile) southwest of Wendover. From Wendover travel west on minor road to Princes Risborough. Take first left then first left again. At top of hill car park is on left.	SP 852062
Wendover public car park	SP 868077
Pitstone Hill car park east of Tring. From sharp bend on B488, 1 km (0.5 miles) southeast of Ivinghoe, take minor road signposted Aldbury. Car park is on right after 1 km (0.5 miles	SP 955149)
National Trust car park for Ivinghoe Beacon, on the left of minor road to Ringshall, 1 km (0.5 miles) south off the B489	SP 962162

Toilets

Place	Map Grid Reference
Princes Risborough (Horn Mill Car Park)	SP 809033
Wendover (Library Car Park)	SP 868078

Police

Oxfordshire and Buckinghamshire	08458 505505
Hertfordshire	01707 354000

Hospitals

Place	Telephone Number	Address
Aylesbury	01296 315000	Stoke Mandeville Hospital, Mandeville Road, Aylesbury.

Vets

Place	Name	Telephone Number
Princes Risborough	Sprinz and Nash	01844 345655
Aylesbury	Hampden Veterinary Hospital (equine)	01296 432633
Wendover	Wendover Heights Veterinary Centre	01296 623439
Tring	Springwell Veterinary Surgery	01442 822151

Farriers

Place	Name	Telephone Number
Aylesbury	A Speller	01296 393896
Berkhamsted	Mark Rudge	01442 879472

Saddlers

Place	Name	Telephone Number
Long Crendon	Crendon Saddlery	01844 208577
Walters Ash	Shana Saddle Shop	01494 564238
Princes Risborough	Beryl P Forrest Saddlery	01494 488130
Chartridge (near The Lee)	Chris Gohl	01494 837138

Bike Repairs

Place	Name	Telephone Number
Princes Risborough	Boltons Bikes	01844 345949
High Wycombe	Cycle Care	01494 447908
Aylesbury	Buckingham Bikes	01296 482077
Tring	Mountain Mania	01442 822458
Berkhamsted	Blue Knight Mobile Repairs	01442 842405
Dunstable	Dysons Cycles	01582 665533

Mountain Bike Hire

Place	Name	Telephone Number
Princes Risborough	Boltons Bikes	01844 345949

Tourist Information Centres

★ offers accommodation booking service

Place	Address/Opening Hours
★ Thame (★ Visitors to office only)	Market House, North Street, Thame OX9 3HH **T/F**: 01844 212834 Opening hours: All year: Mon-Fri 09:30-17:00, Sat 10:00-16:00
Princes Risborough	Tower Court, Horns Lane, Princes Risborough HP27 0AJ **T**: 01844 274795 **F**: 01844 275795 Opening hours: All year: Mon-Fri 09:00-17:00
★ Wendover (★ until 15:30)	Clock Tower, High Street, Wendover HP22 6OU **T**: 01296 696759 **F**: 01296 622460 Opening hours: All year: Mon-Sat 10:00-16:00
Tring	99 Akeman Street, Tring HP23 6AA **T/F**: 01442 823347 **E**: tring@mildram.co.uk Opening hours: All year: Mon-Fri 09:30-15:00, Sat 10:00-13:00
Berkhamsted	Visitor Information Point, c/o Berkhamsted Library, Kings Road, Berkhamsted HP4 3BD **T**: 01438 737333 (ask for Berkhamsted Library) Opening hours: All year: Mon 09:30-17:30, Tue 10:30-20:00, Wed closed, Thu 09:30-20:00, Fri 09:30-18:00, Sat 09:30-16:00
Dunstable	c/o Dunstable Library, Vernon Place, Dunstable LU5 4HA **T**: 01582 471012 **F**: 01582 471290 Opening hours: All year: Mon-Fri 10:00-16:00, Sat 09:30-16:00

Monument on Coombe Hill above Wendover

Walkers on Ivinghoe Beacon

BLEDLOW

 SP7702  1km (0.6miles)
🚂 Princes Risborough 3km
(2miles) 📞

🍺 [||||||||||||] ✕ [||||||||||||]
    S M T W T F S   S M T W T F S

LODGE HILL

SP7900  on path
🚂 Princes Risborough 3km
(2miles)

GR SU787000 100m from Ridgeway
Mr & Mrs C J Gee
Wigans Lane, Bledlow Ridge, High
Wycombe HP14 4BH
T: 01844 344416 **F:** 01844 344703
E: oldcallow@aol.com
www.chilternscottage.co.uk
 1 £40 1 £48 (£25) 🚼
 V 🔥 🚫 🚲 DRY 🔘 ♿ ◆◆◆◆

SAUNDERTON LEE

SP7901  1km (0.6miles)
🚂 Saunderton 2km (1.2miles)

🍺 [||||||||||||] ✕ [||||||||||||]
    S M T W T F S   S M T W T F S

Caring for the Chilterns

You can help the Chilterns by

The Chilterns
Area of Outstanding Natural Beauty

- Enjoying, understanding and caring for the chilterns
- Leaving your car at home
- Showing respect to other users of the countryside
- Supporting the local economy - buy local products and services
- Not disrupting the activities of those who make their living from the countryside
- Taking pride in the Chilterns - follow the Country Code

BRADENHAM

SU8297 5km (3.1miles)
Saunderton 2km (1miles)

S M T W T F S × S M T W T F S

YHA Bradenham — *phone ahead*

The Manager
The Village Hall, Bradenham, High
Wycombe HP14 4HF
T: 01494 562929 **F:** 01494 564743
E: bradenham@yha.org.uk
Dormitory
accommodation, price on application

PRINCES RISBOROUGH

SP8003 on path
Princes Risborough Market
town with full range of services

Coppins — *closed Xmas & New Year*

Mrs Jill Thomas
New Road, Princes Risborough HP27
0LA
T: 01844 344508 **M:** 07745 596103
E: jillthomas@thecoppins.co.uk
2 £45 (£30) (over 10 years)
V

The Black Prince Hotel

Miss C Ling
86 Wycombe Road, Princes Risborough
HP27 0EN
T: 01844 345569 **M:** 07743 453507
F: 01844 345076
3 £55 2 £55 (£35) 3 £35
V
Mastercard, Visa, Delta

View from Whiteleaf Hill above Princes Risborough

HADDENHAM

SP7408 🥾 7.5km (4.6miles)

🚆 Haddenham & Thame Parkway 📞

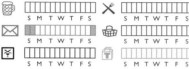

S M T W T F S   S M T W T F S

S M T W T F S   S M T W T F S

S M T W T F S   S M T W T F S

☆ Haddenham Museum
T: 01844 290791
www.haddenham.net

Cover Point

Mrs Pamela Collins
19 The Croft, Haddenham HP17 8AS
T: 01844 290093
E: pam@coverpoint.plus.com

🛏 1 £50 🍴 1 £50 (£35) 🚭 👫 📷
V 🏇 🚲 DRY 📷 🚗

WHITELEAF

SP8204 🥾 1km (0.6miles)

🚆 Monks Risborough 1.5km (1mile)

🍺 ⬜⬜⬜⬜⬜⬜⬜⬜⬜ 🍴 ⬛⬜⬜⬜⬜⬜⬜⬜⬜

S M T W T F S   S M T W T F S

LOWER CADSDEN

SP8204 🥾 on path

🚆 Monks Risborough 2km (1miles)

S M T W T F S   S M T W T F S

ASKETT

SP8105 🥾 2km (1.2miles)

🚆 Monks Risborough 1km (0.5miles)

S M T W T F S   S M T W T F S

Solis Ortu

Mrs Pamela Crockett
Aylesbury Road, Askett, Princes Risborough HP27 9LY
T: 01844 344175/347777 **F:** 01844 343509 **E:** crockett@bucksnet.co.uk

🛏 1 £45 🍴 1 £45 (£25) 🚭 👫 (5 years) V 🏇 🚲 ◆◆◆

GREAT KIMBLE

SU8206 🥾 1km (0.6miles)

🚆 Little Kimble 1km (0.5miles) 📞

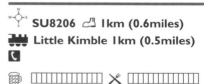

S M T W T F S   S M T W T F S

BUTLERS CROSS

 SP8407 1km (0.6miles)

 Little Kimble 2km (1miles) 📞

 ▓▓░░░░░░░░░ ▓▓░░░░░░░░
   S M T W T F S   S M T W T F S

WENDOVER

SP8607 on path

Wendover 🅗

Market town with full range of services

☆ Wendover Woods
T: 01420 520212
www.forestry.gov.uk

Dunsmore Edge *closed Xmas & New Year*

⌖ GR SP875057 1.6km(1mile) from
Ridgeway
Mr & Mrs Ron & Ursula Drackford
Dunsmore Lane, London Road,
Wendover HP22 6PN
T: 01296 623080 E: uron@lineone.net
🛏 3 £45 🛏 1 £53 (£25) 🚭 ♀♂ V
🔥 🚲 DRY 🚗 👣 ◆◆◆
🅷 En-suite available

Mrs MacDonald's *closed Xmas*

Mr G MacDonald
46 Lionel Avenue, Wendover HP22 6LP
T: 01296 623426
🛏 1 £50 (£25) 🛏 2 £25 🚭 ♀♂ 📺 V
🔥 🚲 DRY 📺 🚗 👣 ◆◆◆

Bacombe Hill west of Wendover

90

WESTON TURVILLE

SP8611 🥾 3km (1.9miles)
🚆 Wendover 4km (2miles) 📞

🍺 |||||||||| ✕ ||||||||||
   S M T W T F S   S M T W T F S
🧺 ||||||||||
   S M T W T F S

The Hamlet B & B

Mrs Maria Burgess
3 Home Close, Weston Turville,
Aylesbury HP22 5SP
T: 01296 612660 **M:** 07889 247903
F: 01296 612660
E: gburg27705@aol.com
🛏 1 £50 🛏 1 £50 (£35) 🛏 1 £25
🚭 VISA Mastercard, Visa, Delta ◆◆◆
🍴 Breakfast not included in price of
room. En-suite available

ST LEONARDS

SP9107 🥾 1.5km (0.9miles)
🚆 Wendover 5km (3miles) 📞

🍺 |||||||||| ✕ ||||||||||
   S M T W T F S   S M T W T F S

Field Cottage *closed Xmas & New Year*

GR SP900063 1km from Ridgeway
Mrs Susan Jepson
St Leonards, Tring HP23 6NS
T: 01494 837602 **F:** 01494 837137
E: michael.jepson@lineone.net
🛏 1 £55 🛏 1 £55 (£40) 🛏 1 £35
🚭 👫 (over 12 years) 📱 V 🚲 DRY
◆◆◆◆ 🍴 VisitBritain Silver Award

CHOLESBURY

SP9307 🥾 4km (2.5miles)
🚆 Tring 7km (4.5miles) 📞

🍺 |||||||||| ✕ ||||||||||
   S M T W T F S   S M T W T F S

Cholesbury House *Closed Xmas & New Year* ♻

Mrs Carol Peebles
Shire Lane, Cholesbury,
Tring HP23 6NA
T: 01494 757123 **F:** 01494 757246
E: carol@cholesburyhouse.co.uk
www.cholesburyhouse.co.uk
🛏 1 £70 (£45) 🚭 V 🦽 🚭 🚲 DRY
🚗 🚶
♻ 2 £5 🍴 Grazing only in Summer

The Greyhound, Aldbury

91

WIGGINTON

SP9310 🥾 **on path**
🚂 **Tring 2km (1miles)** 📞

 |||||||||||||
S M T W T F S ✕ |||||||||||||
S M T W T F S

Rangers Cottage

Mrs Sally Dawson
Tring Park, Wigginton, Tring HP23 6EB
T: 01442 890155 **F:** 01442 827814
E: rangerscottage@aol.com
www.rangerscottage.com

 2 £63 🛏 1 £63 (£48) 🚭 ⚥ V
🚲 DRY VISA Mastercard, Visa ◆◆◆◆
♿ Self-catering accommodation from £80

TRING

SP9211 🥾 **2km (1.2miles)**
🚂 ♿

Small town with range of services

☆ The Walter Rothschild Zoological
Museum
T: 020 79426171
www.nhm.ac.uk/museum/tring

ALDBURY

SP9612 🥾 **1km (0.6miles)**
🚂 **Tring 1.5km (1mile)** 📞

||||||||||| ✕ |||||||||||
S M T W T F S   S M T W T F S
✉ ||||||||||| 🧺 |||||||||||
S M T W T F S   S M T W T F S
☕ |||||||||||
S M T W T F S

☆ Ashridge Estate
T: 01442 842488

16 Stoneycroft

Mrs Sandra Crannage
Aldbury, Tring HP23 5RL
T: 01442 851294 **M:** 07801 846351
F: 01442 851294

🛏 1 £35 (£23) 🛏 1 £23 🚭 ⚥ 📺 V
🔥 🚲 DRY 🥾

PITSTONE

SP9315 🥾 **2.5km (1.6miles)**
🚂 **Tring 4km (2miles)** 📞

 ||||||||||| 🧺 |||||||||||
S M T W T F S   S M T W T F S
☆ Pitstone Green Museum

☆ Pitstone Windmill
T: 01494 528051

IVINGHOE

 SP9416 ⛺ 1.5km (0.9miles)
🚂 Tring 5km (3miles) ☎

| 🍺 | S M T W T F S | ✕ | S M T W T F S |
| 📧 | S M T W T F S | ⚑ | S M T W T F S |

☆ Ivinghoe Watermill
T: 01582 600391

🏠 **YHA Ivinghoe** *phone ahead*
The Manager
The Old Brewery House, High Street,
Ivinghoe LU7 9EP
T: 01296 668251 **F:** 01296 662903
E: ivinghoe@yha.org.uk
🚭 🚶 V 🏕 🌓 🚲 DRY VISA
Mastercard, Visa, Delta
🛏 Dormitory/private accommodation
from £11.80/adult

EDLESBOROUGH

 SP9719 ⛺ 3km (1.9miles)
🚂 Tring 9km (6miles) ☎

| 🍺 | S M T W T F S | ✕ | S M T W T F S |
| 📧 | S M T W T F S | 🧺 | S M T W T F S |

Ridgeway End *closed Xmas*
Mrs Judith Lloyd
5 Ivinghoe Way, Edlesborough,
Dunstable LU6 2EL
T: 01525 220405 **M:** 07721 027339
F: 01525 220405
E: judy.lloyd@tesco.net
🛏 1 £48 🛏 1 £48 🛏 1 £48 (£28)
🚭 🚶 V 🏕 🚲 DRY 🚗 🐾

View from Ivinghoe Beacon

Ivinghoe Beacon from Pitstone Hill

Aldbury

Aldbury	92	Liddington	43
Aldworth	60	Lockeridge	37
Ardington	57	Lodge Hill	87
Ashbury	45	Lower Cadsden	89
Askett	89	Marlborough	37
Aston Rowant	77	Moulsford-on-Thames	60
Avebury	38	North Stoke	72
Barbury Castle	41	Nuffield	75
Benson	74	Ogbourne St George	42
Bishopstone	44	Park Corner	75
Bledlow	87	Pitstone	92
Blewbury	59	Postcombe	77
Bradenham	88	Princes Risborough	88
Britwell Salome	75	St Leonards	91
Broad Hinton	38	Saunderton	87
Butlers Cross	90	South Stoke	71
Chalgrove	76	Sparsholt	55
Childrey	56	Streatley	60
Chilton	58	Swindon	41
Chinnor	78	Tring	92
Chiseldon	41	Uffington	46
Cholesbury	91	Upton	59
Compton	59	Wallingford	73
Crowell	78	Wanborough	43
Crowmarsh Gifford	72	Wantage	56
East Hendred	58	Watlington	76
East Ilsley	58	Wendover	90
Edlesborough	93	West Hendred	57
Faringdon	46	West Ilsley	58
Goring-on-Thames	71	Weston Turville	91
Great Kimble	89	West Overton	38
Haddenham	89	Whiteleaf	89
Henton	78	Wigginton	92
Ivinghoe	93	Winterbourne Bassett	38
Kingston Blount	78	Winterbourne Monkton	38
Kingston Lisle	55	Woolstone	45
Letcombe Regis	56	Wroughton	41
Lewknor	77		

Distances between places along the The Ridgeway in miles

Overton Hill	Ogbourne St George	Fox hill	Uffington Castle	A338 (Wantage)	Bury Down	Streatley	Mongewell Park	Nuffield	Watlington	Chinnor	Princes Risborough	Wendover	Wigginton	Ivinghoe Beacon
Overton Hill														
9.1	Ogbourne St George													
16.5	7.4	Fox hill												
21.9	12.8	5.4	Uffington Castle											
28.2	19.1	11.7	6.3	A338 (Wantage)										
33.9	24.8	17.4	12.0	5.7	Bury Down									
42.0	32.9	25.5	20.1	13.8	8.1	Streatley								
47.7	38.6	31.2	25.8	19.5	13.8	5.7	Mongewell Park							
51.7	42.6	35.2	29.8	23.5	17.8	9.7	4.0	Nuffield						
57.1	48.0	40.6	35.2	28.9	23.2	15.1	9.4	5.4	Watlington					
62.7	53.6	46.2	40.8	34.5	28.8	20.7	15.0	11.0	5.6	Chinnor				
68.0	58.9	51.5	46.1	39.8	34.1	26.0	20.3	16.3	10.9	5.3	Princes Risborough			
73.9	64.8	57.4	52.0	45.7	40.0	31.9	26.2	22.2	16.8	11.2	5.9	Wendover		
80.0	70.9	63.5	58.1	51.8	46.1	38.0	32.3	28.3	22.9	17.3	12.0	6.1	Wigginton	
85.5	76.4	69.0	63.6	57.3	51.6	43.5	37.8	33.8	28.4	22.8	17.5	11.6	5.5	Ivinghoe Beacon